*"Never forget that
I am with you every day."*

Matthew 28:20 (TPT)

THE EMOTIONAL DEVOTIONAL: FOLLOWING JESUS IN EVERY EMOTION
WRITTEN BY TEENAGE GIRLS, FOR TEENAGE GIRLS.

© *2021 Justin Rossow and Next Step Press*
ISBN: 9798579155085 · Imprint: Independently published

Edited by Justin Rossow
Assistant Editor, Naomi Rossow

Written for teenage girls, by teenage girls:
Naomi Rossow (19)
Gabriella Wiechman (18)
Elizabeth Rossow (17)
Katherine Rossow (14)
Eliana Wiechman (13)

Illustrations and Mood Trackers: Lucie Orozco (17)
Title credit: Josiah Wiechman (15)

Inquiries or comments may be directed to
Curator@findmynextstep.org.

We help you take a next step

THE EMOTIONAL DEVOTIONAL

Following Jesus in every emotion

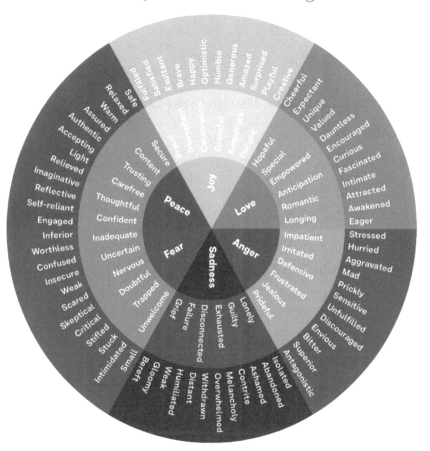

by teenage girls, for teenage girls

Table of Contents

JOY

SADNESS

LOVE

A Note to Family and Friends by Justin Rossow

If you are not a teenage girl, this book was not written for you. You can still read it, of course, and you would discover a lot about yourself, about teenage girls, and even about following Jesus in your emotions. But it's not really *for you.*

That's not to say your emotions aren't important, or teenage girls are somehow more emotional than other people. God created all of us human beings as people with bodies and souls, minds and emotions. All of us can learn more and more to follow Jesus in every emotion.

The teenagers who wrote this book share their experience from their own particular perspective with an honesty that invites especially other teenage girls into the wonderful and confusing process of inviting Jesus into their emotions. They write with authenticity and empathy, as a friend for someone who could really use a friend right now.

This Emotional Devotional isn't trying to "fix" or "cure" anything about the teenage girl in your life. The one thing this book *will* do is help her practice bringing her emotions to Jesus and talking to Him about them.

That might sound simple, but growing into a personal and confidential relationship with Jesus is part of what it means to become a person of faith. That dependence on Jesus in the midst of every experience—even those that make faith seem foolish or juvenile—is something we all will continue to grow into, until our faith is made sight. But we don't have to walk that journey alone.

The list of emotions covered here is not complete. How could it be? But these emotions are diverse and common enough to cultivate the habit of looking for Jesus in every emotion.

I love the girls who wrote this book. They risk sharing their inner thoughts and prayers and struggles and failures so that others might also think and pray and struggle and fail *with Jesus* instead of on their own.

If you give this book as a gift to the important teenage girl in your life, don't expect a sudden miracle; but do expect for her—little by little, one step at a time—to begin to feel more confident bringing her experiences to Jesus, even when she doesn't know what to pray.

And expect Jesus to be there for her, before she prays, while she prays, and when she forgets to pray. That, by far, is miracle enough.

A Note to Teenage Girls by Naomi Rossow

As a teenage girl, you experience a multitude of emotions every day in different combinations and presentations. Emotions are so unpredictable, especially for teenagers. As you grow in your body and mind, you also want to also be able to grow in your faith.

The changes that happen in your life over the course of these years can be scary and confusing, especially if you don't have someone to walk through it with you. As the oldest child, oldest cousin, in a new school and state, I often felt alone in the changes I was experiencing. A few years later, I now talk to my little sister and get to help her walk through the mood swings and outbursts of being a teenage girl. Sometimes it helps to know you are not alone.

The teenage girls who wrote this devotion book know firsthand what it's like to wade through the waves of emotion. In fact, we are wading through them right now, too. These devotions are not meant to be therapy or counseling. We haven't gone through medical school. None of us holds a degree in psychology. The book is not a "fix" for your emotions. We just want to help you invite Jesus into your emotions. We want to share our stories with openness, honesty, and vulnerability, in hopes that we can help you grow in your faith and build a stronger relationship with Jesus.

The list of emotions in this book is far from complete; but it is a start. So, when you are ready, read on and see how we have experienced inviting Jesus into our emotions.

You are not alone in your journey.

Let's do this!

Section 1:

Practicing Prayer

Learning to Pray

This activity is designed to help you be more comfortable with your own personal prayer. In the church, there seems to be a "right" way to pray, with fancy words, long sentences, a proper beginning and end, and even a special order. While this churchy prayer is, of course, not wrong, it's not the only way to pray.

Matthew 6:7 (MSG)

"Find a quiet, secluded place so you won't be tempted to role-play before God. Just be there as simply and honestly as you can manage. The focus will shift from you to God, and you will begin to sense his grace."

Practicing Prayer by Naomi Rossow

Prayer is a communication between you and your Father, Friend, and Savior. Think of prayer as a conversation, rant, heart-to-heart, or chat with a close friend instead of a speech performed for the principal.

When you start to practice, find a quiet place to be alone. You don't have to be alone (or quiet) every time you pray, and, in fact, you shouldn't be. But, for now, we are learning and getting comfortable with the feeling of opening up, so find a safe place to run this prayer experiment.

I am going to lead you through a series of questions and exercises with the goal of helping you feel more comfortable talking to Jesus as a friend. Feel free to go through this activity as many times as you want. Prayer is not a one-time thing, and it gets easier as you continue to do it. I mean, practice makes perfect, right?

When you are ready, turn to the next page and open your heart to your Heavenly Father. Again, I find Matthew 6 to be helpful:

> *"This is your Father you are dealing with, and he knows better than you what you need. With a God like this loving you, you can pray very simply"* (Matthew 6:9, MSG).

A Simple Prayer Experiment

1. Find somewhere comfortable and quiet to either sit or stand, whatever you are more comfortable with.

2. Take a deep breath and close your eyes. Breathe in for five seconds, hold it for another five, and then release it for another five. Do this at least once, but feel free to do it more. This will allow you to center yourself, your emotions, and your thoughts. I find it is very helpful to do this anytime I start to feel overwhelmed or stressed.

3. Feel free to keep your eyes closed or to have them open; whatever is comfortable for you. Extend your arms so they are in an open, inviting position. Let your hands relax so your palms are facing up and open in a sign of dependence and acceptance.

4. Take another deep breath and open your heart and mind to your God. Invite the Spirit to be present.

5. Now, just start talking.

    You don't have to have a formal opening. You don't need an agenda. Just word-vomit to your Father who loves you unconditionally. Simply talk for as long as you want or need. This will feel uncomfortable and awkward at first, but as you continue it will come more naturally.

6. As you finish, use any closing you wish, or simply stop talking. Your words have been heard.

Congratulations! You just had a meaningful conversation with your Friend who will never leave you. What's more, God can't wait to hear from you again, so don't be a stranger!

You Can't Scare God Away

Oftentimes it feels like our emotions are too big for us to handle; but that doesn't apply to God. God loves to hear about all our emotions, no matter how intense. Sometimes we just need a reminder that God can handle all the things we feel.

You're Not Too Big for God by Gabriella Wiechman

I've always been what people call a "big personality." This is a nice way of saying I'm loud and show a lot of emotions. I've been this way my whole life, and I never really learned to hide who I was until a few years ago.

A few years ago I started to spend a lot more time around my peers. I had always been home-schooled, so spending a lot of time around the same people was kind of new to me. They saw every part of me because I didn't know how to wear a mask.

Most people cover up who they are around certain people or in certain places, but I hadn't spent much time anywhere besides church and home, so I hadn't experienced that as much. Now I was spending all of my time around people who naturally did this every day, so for the first time I wasn't sure how much of me I wanted to be.

I learned how to tone down who I was when I became overwhelming to other people. When I was "disrupting the peace" I had to learn how to be "just a little less me." They weren't comfortable with how passionate I was or how loud I laughed, so they judged me. When someone would tell me I was weird it made me want to hide that part of me. Slowly but surely I learned how to cover up who I was, whether I wanted to or not.

This happens a lot in our culture. People are constantly trying to tell us how to change. Maybe you should eat some more, or maybe you should start a diet. Maybe you should hit the gym, or maybe you should take a break from the weights. Or maybe it isn't about your looks, maybe it's more personal and it's about who you are and what you do. Maybe you should go to college, or maybe you need to pick a different college. Maybe you care too much, or maybe you should care more.

The maybes could go on and on, because other people will never run out of things to change about you. That's because everyone is different, their opinions and standards are different from every other person's, but most importantly they are different from God's. God has a different set of standards we are held to, but God also has a different capability to forgive and give grace.

We are constantly trying to gain approval from other people. We end up muffling our true personalities. I picture it like this:

> Before you learn how to cover up who you are, you are like a little girl running around, dancing and twirling in a pretty dress. Then people start to tell you to change who you are and your smile starts to fade, but you still stay mostly true to yourself. One day someone says something about how you look, who you are, or what you do, and they try to change you again. This is the last one, you can't take any more suggestions on how to edit who you are, so you change. Those people who are telling you who to be and how to act are muffling your personality like someone holding their hand over your mouth so you can't breathe. They are suffocating your personality. The more you listen to their suggestions, the less you are able to breathe and be true to who you are.
>
> You don't feel like yourself anymore, but you keep changing and adapting because you want to please them, because it would be "too selfish" to do something for yourself. It would be "too disrespectful" to laugh too loud. They say you're too ugly when you smile, and you want to make sure no one feels uncomfortable, so you just don't smile. But then you frown too much and you look depressed, so you soft smile so no one knows how hurt you actually are inside.

This is an issue every girl I've ever talked to has struggled with on a certain level. We all go through this same thing: we feel like we have to change to be loved. We can't have a personality that's "too big" or "too small" because someone is going to be uncomfortable.

But God created you with emotions. God created you with a personality. God designed you knowing that you would feel this way, and your Heavenly Father is OK with that! God loves your big smile and your loud laugh; your soft smile and twinkling eyes.

God created you to feel how big you feel or how small you feel. God created you to talk as much or as little as you do. God created you to smile as big or as small as you do. God has called you to do the work you were created to do, even though other people will tell you that your calling is weird or not good enough. God created you; God loves you, the real you; and God loves who you are becoming.

Other people will always tell us that we are too big or too much, but God never will. Jesus will never once turn you away or tell you He doesn't want to hear from you.

I've found myself feeling like I can't be mad at God because God can't take my anger. Or I feel like I can't get too excited about what's happening in my life because to God those things are just too small. When that's written out it sounds pretty ridiculous, right? How could the God who created the entire universe and who defeated death itself not be able to handle my bad days?

What I've done is I've taken the things people have told me about what or how I feel and *I've assumed that's how God feels about me, too.* I've assumed that God can only take a certain amount of *me* before I become too much. I've assumed God doesn't care about the exciting things in my life. I've assumed all of these things, but that's not how God feels about me.

In 2 Corinthians 12:9 the Lord says to Paul, *"My grace is sufficient for you, for my power is made perfect in weakness."*

Jesus feels the same way about me. Jesus can take my anger because He has grace. Jesus can handle me yelling at Him in frustration because His grace is sufficient to cover over that. Jesus wants to hear the things that frustrate me because He wants to show me His grace that covers over everything.

> *"You have searched me, LORD, and you know me ... For you created my inmost being; you knit me together in my mother's womb. I praise you because I am fearfully and wonderfully made; your works are wonderful, I know that full well.*

6

My frame was not hidden from you when I was made in the secret place, when I was woven together in the depths of the earth. Your eyes saw my unformed body; all the days ordained for me were written in your book before one of them came to be."

Psalm 139:1, 13-16 (NIV)

God can handle your emotions. God embraces who you are because that's exactly who God created you to be. Jesus knows every part of you and He still loves you! Everything you've ever done and everything you ever will do God knew when you were created, and God still chose to create you because you have something to offer.

So God can handle your emotions. God loves to hear your anger and your excitement. God can deal with your fear and your shame. Your joy is not too big; your failure is not too embarrassing; your dreams are not too silly; your temper-tantrum is not too childish. God simply loves you. The real you. The best and worst of who you are. Jesus thought you were worth dying for; how will He not love you completely, no matter what?

Let us run with endurance the race that is set before us, looking to Jesus, the founder and perfecter of our faith, who for the joy that was set before him endured the cross, despising the shame, and is seated at the right hand of the throne of God.

Hebrews 12:1-2 (ESV)

"The joy that was set before Him." That's you! Jesus thinks you are so unique, and valuable, and amazing, and special that He thought you were worth the cross. You! You don't have to be perfect, you are already loved.

So keep feeling those big feelings, keep smiling big and laughing loud, because God created you knowing every quirk and every part of you that other people would judge. Jesus knows your best and your worst, and He still said the cross was worth it if the cross meant He gets to be with you.

Jesus is up to something in your life. The Spirit is leading you and guiding you and shaping you. Your emotions can sometimes give you an insight into what God is doing in your life.

Praying the Emotion Wheel by Gabriella Wiechman

Oftentimes, we feel more than one emotion at a time, or what we are feeling seems to be a bit of several different emotions all mixed together. This can make it hard, confusing, and honestly overwhelming to try and figure out what we are actually feeling. God created us as complex creatures, on purpose, so it is important to invite our Creator into our emotions as we try and dig deeper into what we are feeling and why.

If you look at the cover of this book, you will see a wheel with six sections and three layers. This is the emotions wheel. A lot of times our emotions can be very confusing, and it can be difficult to put a finger on the exact thing (or things) you are feeling. So I'm here to help walk you through this tool so you can begin to identify more clearly what you are feeling.

The Center of the Wheel

At the center of the wheel, you will see six broad categories of emotions: love, joy, peace, fear, sadness, and anger. Oftentimes for me it is easier to start with these more general emotions to find out what I'm really feeling rather than starting with something more specific.

To help you identify the general emotion you are experiencing, you might find it helpful to look at your body language. How fast or slow is your heart beating? What does your face look like? Are you smiling? Frowning? Scowling? Are your muscles tense or relaxed? How is your language; the way you are speaking to and interacting with others? Is your breath slow and controlled, or quick and excited?

These are some of the questions I ask myself, or the things I try to notice in my body as I try to pinpoint the things I'm feeling. It also helps you to slow down and pay attention to your body (something we don't usually do in our crazy lives). So something as simple as noticing your breath and heartbeat can be very helpful in identifying what emotions you are feeling.

The Second Layer and the Outside Ring

Moving out from the center of the emotions wheel, you'll find a layer with more specific emotions that fall under each of the six broader categories. We wrote devotions for each of these 36 emotions to help you pinpoint more exactly what you are feeling.

Keep in mind, though, there are thousands of emotions a human can feel, and we have only covered 36 of them! To help you start to notice more of the emotions you feel, we also added an outer ring to the wheel with some more specific examples related to the six general emotions. Naming your emotion can be one helpful step to experiencing your emotion in healthy ways. Don't stress if you don't find your exact emotion on our list. You can name it whatever you want (even if you have to make up a word!). But thinking through what you are feeling can really help.

The Process

To give you an idea of how to use the emotion wheel, I am going to walk you through my process.

When I am noticing myself getting overwhelmed with emotions or confused as to what I am feeling, the first thing I always try to do (but sometimes forget) is to sit in God's presence. For me this looks like turning on worship music with the volume all the way up, putting away my phone and any other devices, and turning off the lights.

Sometimes I just sit or lie down, and other times I'm jumping around worshipping; there is no right or wrong way to sit with Jesus. I like to listen to music because it helps me drown out other distractions and focus on Jesus and what He is telling me.

Once I have soaked in Christ's presence for a little while, I then try to notice what my body has been doing during the day. Am I relaxed, or have my muscles been tense? Have I been short tempered, or have small things not bothered me? Things like that help me notice which of the broader six emotions I am feeling. Most people already have experience naming these broad emotions, so you might find it easy to pick one, two, or even three you are feeling right now.

From there it becomes a bit more personal and complicated because there are so many emotions we could be feeling, and not just one at a time. So this is the part where it is so important to have Jesus in the conversation (just like every other part), because through Christ I find myself being made more aware of what it is I'm feeling.

For me, I usually hear God's voice in my mind very clearly, and maybe you do too! That often is what helps me understand the deeper and more complex emotions I'm feeling, but sometimes God's voice seems distant and hard to hear, and that's okay!

When I am having trouble hearing God's voice in the midst of my emotions, or my mind is so loud I can't seem to focus, it is helpful to me to just look at a list of emotions. I go through the list and read an emotion word and think about what it means and if that sounds like what I'm feeling, just like you might do if you are hungry and want a snack—you might go and look at your options. It's just the same with emotions. There might not be a list of all the emotions you could ever feel, but that's what the emotions wheel is for: take a look at your options and see if any of them seem like what you are feeling.

Then, once I figure out the emotion (or usually, emotions) I am feeling, I take it to God. I ask God to comfort me if I'm afraid, or celebrate with me if I'm excited. No matter what emotion you are feeling, your Heavenly Father will always want to know about it and talk to you about it.

I invite you to take a look at the emotions wheel and become familiar with at least the six general emotions so that the next time you are confused or overwhelmed with your feelings, you are able to use this tool to help you distinguish what you are feeling. Then invite Jesus into the very specific experience of your very specific emotions. He'll be glad to meet you there!

Reflect, Record, Respond by Naomi Rossow

This short activity might help you get used to identifying what you are feeling. For some people, this comes really easily, and others have to try harder; but everyone can do it.

St. Ignatius of Loyola (who lived a few hundred years ago) came up with a five-step reflection to help people prayerfully consider their emotions with Jesus … which just happens to be very similar to our goal in this book. The five steps he came up with were something like:

- Become aware of God's presence
- Review your day with gratitude
- Notice your emotions with Jesus
- Prayerfully consider events of the day
- Look toward tomorrow

I have simplified this down to three steps you can do before you get in bed tonight, or after school before tackling your homework, or after dinner. Whatever time works best for you, take five minutes or so and walk through these steps to reflect on your day and emotions.

Use the calendar below to record a week's worth of emotions. You might be able to see a pattern or a recurring theme. Sometimes it helps to know you've been excited all week, or sad for the last three days, or really up and down in your emotions. Don't limit each day to a single emotion; try to capture the most relevant feelings you experienced. And wonder with Jesus what the Spirit was doing in your life each day.

Reflect

The process of self-reflection might be new or awkward to you. This is completely normal. Give it some time for your mind to adjust. Let your mind wander for a few minutes. Get comfortable. Take a few deep breaths and acknowledge the presence of God with you. Briefly look back on your day with Jesus. As you do this short reflection, notice the emotions that stick out to you from your day.

Record

As you reflect on your day, record those emotions on the calendar provided on the next page. Start to name those emotions with Jesus. It can be hard to identify exactly what you felt that day. Don't punish yourself if you can only come up with one or two. That is okay! The important part is naming your emotions with Jesus. Repeat this activity every day for a week.

You can easily repeat this experiment with a calendar or journal of your own. Check out the Mood Trackers in Section 3 and try recording your emotions for a whole month. See what you learn about yourself and about what Jesus is doing in your life!

Respond

Respond to the list of emotions you made. Just as you reflected on your day's emotions, see if you can identify the root of each emotion. Invite Jesus to be part of this response.

Consider the events of the day. What experience triggered those emotions? You might not be able to identify a specific reason for your emotions, and the reasons you do find might not be logical. That's okay. In fact, it's normal!

As you process your emotions, open your heart to the work of the Holy Spirit. Maybe you will feel there is a clear next step as you respond to your emotions. Maybe that next step is simply to continue tracking your emotions. Maybe there isn't a clear next step to take. That's okay, too.

Respond to your emotions in whatever way Jesus is leading you to, even if it's simply going to bed. And as you go to bed or finish up what your evening has in store, look toward your day tomorrow. What do you have to do? Is there something special to look forward to? How can you be aware of God in your day tomorrow? How do the emotions you identified just now affect your day tomorrow?

Come back in a month or so and do this activity again to see how your emotions and mindset may have changed.

WED	TUES	MON	SUN
	SAT	FRI	THURS

Listen to God

There have been many times in my life where I wished I could hear God's voice more clearly. I wanted to hear Jesus talk directly to me, but I didn't know how. The thing about hearing God speak is it isn't the same for everyone. Everyone interacts differently with God, so everyone will hear God's voice in a different way.

1 Kings 19:11-13 (NIV)

"The LORD said, 'Go out and stand on the mountain in the presence of the LORD, for the LORD is about to pass by.'

Then a great and powerful wind tore the mountains apart and shattered the rocks before the Lord, but the LORD was not in the wind. After the wind there was an earthquake, but the LORD was not in the earthquake. After the earthquake came a fire, but the LORD was not in the fire. And after the fire came a gentle whisper. When Elijah heard it, he pulled his cloak over his face and went out and stood at the mouth of the cave.

Then a voice said to him, 'What are you doing here, Elijah?'"

Just a Little Whisper by Gabriella Wiechman

I think many times we, myself included, desire for Jesus to speak in some mighty and powerful way. We expect that the Spirit will come in tongues of fire and through roaring winds. And God does ... sometimes. But more often than not I've found that God likes to speak to me through a small voice in my head. It's not always completely comprehensible. It may be a voice, a song, a picture, a dream, but whatever it is, it's God.

The frustrating part is I don't always know it's God. I often worry that I am saying something to myself in my head that I want to be God, but it isn't. So how do you discern which one is God's voice and which one isn't?

That's where it gets tricky, because we all hear God differently. So I wish I could give you a simple "Five Steps to Hearing God's Voice" that would help you understand what God is speaking to you; but I can't.

What I can tell you, though, is that God is constantly speaking to you. Before I was able to hear and discern God's voice, I was disappointed because my parents could. But God has never called us to a life of comparison. God wants to speak to you in a special and unique way, so go to the place where you know you *can* hear from God.

The Bible is God's Word, so when we read from it, that is God speaking to us. Prayer is talking to God, and when we speak, God hears us. Maybe you want to hear God's voice from the sky, like John the Baptist did, but maybe God is wanting to tell you something for only you to hear; something spoken in a still, small whisper.

So I know it can be so hard to listen, especially when you don't know what you are listening for, but I encourage you to keep trying. Try to notice God in everything you do, and everywhere you go. God doesn't just speak through words, the Spirit speaks through people, events, songs, and feelings. Bringing your feelings to God is another step to a deeper relationship with your Father. I find that the closer I get to Christ, the more I begin to notice Him working around me and speaking to me.

I invite you to not restrict how you think Jesus can speak to you, but instead notice all the ways He is at work in your life and talk to God about that. The more you communicate with God, the more you will begin to notice God communicating with you.

My Prayer For You

Let me pray for you.

Father God,
I thank You for the person who is reading this right now. I thank You that You created them with a purpose and a mission for You. I know that right now they are struggling with hearing Your voice, and I ask that You speak loudly in their lives right now. I ask that however You desire, You show up big in their life.

As they are going through this season in their life, I ask that You show them the unique way You want to communicate with them.

Help them to *see You*.

Help them to *feel You*.

Help them to *hear You*.

Father, please help this beautiful daughter of Yours notice Your voice in her life, however Your Word comes to her.

I love You, God.

Amen.

Four Seasons Faith Experiment by Naomi Rossow

Take a moment to reflect on that prayer and the ways you can see Jesus working in your life. On the next page is an activity designed to help you listen for what Jesus is working in your heart. You might not physically hear God's voice while doing this activity, but in listing things God is doing in your life, you can start to see how the Spirit might be speaking in your heart.

The page is divided up into four sections: spring, summer, autumn, and winter. As you add color to the spring section, list things Jesus is starting new in your life. As you add color to the summer section, list things that Jesus is bringing to a bloom in your life, things that are going well. In the autumn section, list things that Jesus is bringing to a close in your life. And, in the winter section, list things that Jesus has let fall inactive and ponder why that might be. Listen rather than talk during this activity. Invite the Holy Spirit into your heart and allow your heart and mind to be led by Jesus.

Spring: What is Jesus starting new in your life?

> *If anyone is in Christ, the new creation has come:*
> *The old has gone, the new is here!*
> *—2 Corinthians 5:17 (NIV)*

Summer: What is Jesus bringing to bloom in your life?

> *If you remain in me and I in you,*
> *you will bear much fruit.*
> *—John 15:5 (NIV)*

Autumn: What is Jesus bringing to a close in your life?

> *"Whoever loses their life for me will find it."*
> *—Matthew 16:25 (NIV)*

Winter: What is Jesus letting fall inactive, and why?

> *"Every branch that does bear fruit [my Father] prunes*
> *so that it will be even more fruitful." —John 15:2 (NIV)*

Following Jesus ...
On Your Period

The miracle of motherhood comes at a price: years of periods and monthly menstrual cycles with raging hormones, confusing emotions, and sudden mood swings. Welcome to the club.

Chocolate, Cramps, and Crying by Naomi Rossow

Take it from a girl who has experienced her period for 7-8 days every month of every year for 7 years: it sucks. Stomach cramps, back pain, messed up appetite, minor cravings, mood swings, tampon/pad changes, bleeding through, swimming complications, crazy hormone levels, heavy flow, light flow, weird flow, being late, irregular patterns, etc. ... It sucks.

Over the course of those 7 years, I have come to terms with how to deal with the pain and struggle of having my monthly period. I think to myself, "You want to have a baby, so this is good. It means you can have a baby one day" ... and then of course, the pain of my stomach and back cramping yells at that statement, reminding me: "It's not time for you to have a baby yet!"

Hormones cause my emotions to go insane and fluctuate for no apparent reason. The same hormones make me want to laugh at something that wasn't funny, cry because of a slight inconvenience, or punch my sister because of small transgressions that would normally get no reaction from me. The same body that loves swimming doesn't want to get in the water because I feel bloated and feel self-conscious in my bathing suit. I lay on the floor to get some relief from the pain in my stomach and back, not wanting to move to get pain meds that would help me function normally again. I don't feel like myself at all; or I feel like myself even more. Sometimes I am more confident than normal, and other times my confidence escapes me.

The entire menstrual cycle is a roller coaster of emotions. A typical cycle for me starts with my period, in all its painful glory. I get a few days' break before ovulation starts and I am full of estrogen, making me more confident and energetic as my body prepares to create a tiny human. I get about a week of normalcy after that. But when my body starts to catch on to the fact that it isn't going to get to do the job it is prepared to do, my body turns into a drama queen and throws a fit. That's when PMS hits. This wonderful week comes with a plethora of symptoms. I am irritable and touchy. My back and stomach cramp and my boobs are sore 24/7. As if that were not enough, the next week my uterus literally tears itself apart in frustration that it isn't housing a tiny human. (Did you know that your period is your uterus shedding its innermost layer?)

God created our bodies so beautifully and intricately that we can conceive, house, and grow another human in them. I love our bodies. They fascinate me and remind me just how incredible our God is. But recognizing the beauty and intricacy of your body doesn't lessen your menstrual pain or make the mood swings less intense.

I get about one and a half weeks of normalcy in my cycle. The majority of the month is taken up by hormones, pain, and blood. And it is different for every person. Some girls cramp so much they can't get out of bed. Some girls get so sick they vomit. Some barely feel the infamous pain.

Emotional responses and triggers change girl to girl, so I can't help you with the specifics. But I can tell you that, whatever crazy emotions your hormones throw on you, you can bring them to Jesus. Jesus wants to be the one you cry to when you have no logical reason to be crying. He wants to be the one you complain to when your cramps keep you in one place and position for the whole day. Jesus wants to be the one to bring you chocolate.

Okay, that last one is a little difficult until the Second Coming, but you get the point. Jesus wants you to be yourself—in all your pain and joy—in front of Him. The Spirit delights in being there with you. The Father enjoys comforting you. So, next time you are on your period and the hormones shoot up and the emotions start flying from one extreme to the other, invite Jesus to be a part of that experience, just as you do in the deeper emotions of big events. Jesus is with you and likes being with you, even on your period. You can do this! And you are definitely not alone.

Prayer

Hey Jesus,

I am on my period this week. I have found it has made me super irritable to the people around me today. I am normally a sociable person, but today I get annoyed by everyone who talks to me. Yesterday it was the opposite, and all I wanted to do was talk to everyone and make new friends.

I feel like I either want to cry, scream, sleep, or laugh, and I don't have a reason for any of them. So, whatever happens next, be with me in it. Come join me in my hormonal emotions.

Okay, I am going to go eat some chocolate now. Bye.

Section 2:

Following Jesus
in Every Emotion

Peace

Secure | Content | Trusting
Carefree | Thoughtful | Confident

Secure

A feeling of calm washes over you and relaxes your body when you feel safe in a place or with a person. When I experience security, my breathing is slower, and I feel in no hurry to move from place to place. I often find that a small smile rests on my face without force. My shoulders relax down and my arms swing freely.

2 Samuel 22:33 (NIV)

"It is God who arms me with strength and keeps my way secure."

My Happy Place by Naomi Rossow

OKAY, let's start with a short activity to get you in the right mood. I want you to imagine yourself in your perfectly peaceful happy place. If you don't know what that is for you, feel free to use mine: I am sitting on the back of the boat with my feet splashing in the cool water of the lake. The sun is starting to set, throwing beautiful shades of pink and orange across the water. I have a light blanket wrapped across my shoulders, and I am in my bathing suit. My boyfriend is sitting next to me with his feet in the water next to mine. His arm is wrapped around my back, and my head is on his shoulder. We sit there happily enjoying the water, each other's presence, and the beautiful sunset.

Wow. How peaceful we can come to be in small moments with the people who we love the most. It's amazing. Take a deep breath and enjoy the moment. This sense of security and peacefulness is a blessing. There are so many things in our life that cause stress and panic. Each day we face questions, but we also receive times of peace. Like in my example, these moments can be shared with someone we love, or they can be experienced alone.

Peacefulness comes when we are feeling happy about something. A new job or a new friendship has your heart light, and in those light moments you feel secure. But I think even more powerful are the moments of security in a storm of chaos. I can remember some key times I have felt secure where I was, even in days of panic: just a simple moment where the fresh air gives me the space to breathe finally; or my mother's comforting hand allows me to regain a sense of belonging and security that had been taken away. Even moments after my siblings woke me up before I wanted to be up, and it resulted in a calm morning of writing.

In the midst of panic, God gives us moments of security. And we breathe. Bring Jesus into these lighter moments, too, just like you bring Him into the heavier emotions you experience. Whether the sunset or sparkling water gives you a moment of peace, recognize the Giver of the gift. Invite Jesus to share it with you. He loves sunsets and sunrises, and Jesus is always glad to spend some time with you.

People Like Me

In 2 Samuel 22, David praises the Lord in the midst of his distress. David recounts how he called upon the Lord and stayed faithful in times of trial. He reminds us that we are guided by the Lord. David suffered through capture. He faced panic. He faced fear. He faced distress. He faced hopelessness. He faced all these things which we experience in our lives. He did it in the name of the Lord, just as we do. And he also knew security. He knew peace.

David reveled in the peace of the Lord, secure in the love of his Father. When you feel secure, you are not alone.

Prayer

Feel free to change or add to this prayer or any of the prayers in this book. They are intended to help you express what you are feeling to God, as a guide, but there is not a "standard" way to experience or express your emotions.

Wow.

Thank You, God. You are truly wonderful. You give us blessings in the midst of chaos, and You give us times of peace to breathe when life feels like it might fall apart. I am amazed by the security Your love gives me.

Thank You, Lord.

Content

Being content is feeling satisfied or pleased. When you are content you feel cheery and happy. When you're content you are grateful for the way your life is going. You're pleased with it. Sometimes when I am content I just feel like lying down, smiling, and closing my eyes to enjoy the moment.

Luke 12:24 (NIV)

"Consider the ravens: They do not sow or reap, they have no storeroom or barn; yet God feeds them. And how much more valuable you are than birds!"

God Will Provide by Eliana Wiechman

Some days when it's raining, I just go outside and stand in the warm rain, letting it soak through my clothes. I lift my head up to the heavens and relax. I thank God for all of the amazing gifts the Father has given me; even all of the little things, and I realize that my life is really going pretty great. I feel satisfied and complete. I feel well-rested and relaxed. This is what it feels like to be content.

Sometimes it's hard to be content, and sometimes even when we are feeling satisfied, it doesn't stay that way. Will it be like this tomorrow? Will God keep giving these small gifts, and peace?

In Luke 12, Jesus says that God will provide for you, just like God provides for the ravens. No matter how much you have, plenty or little, God will provide. Your Heavenly Father will continue to provide for you every day. You don't have to worry that it won't always be like this (and trust me, it won't). But when you are feeling content, invite Jesus into that feeling with you! Thank Him for the big and small gifts you have been given.

Think of all those gifts God has given you, that peace that you are feeling, and say a prayer of thanksgiving. Your Father has given you so much more than you know, you just don't always see it. God will always be there to provide for you in any and every situation.

"Consider the ravens." God gave them everything they needed to stay alive, and you are so much more important to God than the ravens are! Knowing this, go into your day remembering that God will provide for you through the ups and downs. God continues to give you everything you need to live your life.

People Like Me

In Philippians, Paul the apostle says that he had learned to be content in any and every situation. He knew what it was like to have plenty, and what it was like to have little, but in both he learned to be content. For this, he thanked God, because Paul knew that he could do anything through his Father. Anything is possible for the One who gives us strength.

This was how Paul learned to be content in all situations. He knew that God would provide him with the strength he needed to go on. He knew that he could be content with what God gave him because God would give him all that he needed, nothing less. Knowing this, Paul was content despite horrible situations. When you feel content, you are not alone.

Let's Pray

Dear God,

Thank You so much for the peace You have provided me. Thank You for the love You have lavished on me and the gifts You have given me. Thank You for providing me with the strength to do anything through You, my Father.

Please help me to learn, like Paul, to be content with whatever You have given me in any situation. Send Your Spirit into my heart. Come join me in this peaceful moment of contentment.

I love You. Thank You, Jesus. Amen.

What are some of the people, places, or things that make you feel content?

Trusting

When you feel trusting toward God, you might notice yourself being more comfortable following your calling. When I trust God, I typically hear God's voice more clearly and notice the Spirit working in my life more than normal.

Exodus 14:13-14 (NIV)

"Moses answered the people, 'Do not be afraid. Stand firm and you will see the deliverance the Lord will bring you today. The Egyptians you see today you will never see again. The Lord will fight for you; you need only to be still.'"

A Crazy Step by Gabriella Wiechman

I'm going to be honest, I'm not always super optimistic. But I will say one thing: I have been learning through experience that life is so much more fun when you are constantly expecting God to do amazing things.

Almost six years ago my family did something a little bit abnormal. Well, actually, it was a lot abnormal.

I was 12 years old and I had just begun to build some great connections at my church. I had a job that actually paid pretty well, I had friends that I could hang out with, and I finally felt like I had something to offer at the church. I loved working near my dad in the church office but having my own responsibilities. And on top of all that, my family was living in the nicest house we had ever owned.

What I'm saying is, I had built my community where I felt like I belonged. But God had a different plan (which I'm learning is often the case…). Here's a little clip from my journal the day I found out what God's new path for my family was. (Keep in mind, this is word for word from a 12-year-old.)

> *I'm starting this journal today because I feel a need to express my feelings over these next few tough months (/years?). Tonight my parents told me that Dad quit his job as a pastor at our church.*

He said that he wasn't going to become a pastor anywhere else for a while. This was especially hard for me because he's been a pastor all 12 ½ years of my life. Mom and dad said that even they don't know very many details. They said God was calling us to this new life, and we're answering with a "yes."

We've been reading a book lately called, "God's Smuggler," and it talks about Brother Andrew, and how he gets in the wheel-barrow, and COMPLETELY trusts God with EVERYTHING. I want to be like Andrew, he inspires me greatly. I now have a chance to, so I'm jumpin' in the wheel-barrow (dramatic music) with my whole family to support and to support me on the ride of surprises.

And here is one more, short journal entry from the next morning:

This morning I woke up and I feel the hope and grace of a new day. I'm excited to see how many things I can give away. I'm trying to fill up 3 tote bins. I've just noticed how much stuff God has blessed me with, and now I have a chance to turn around and bless others with my things.

So first off, I should let you know that I have always been quite the dramatic child. But soon this new journey my family was on following God became what we like to call, "The Trust Adventure."

For seven months we drove around the country, all six of us crammed into a white Suburban with a ten-foot trailer pulling behind. We stayed with friends, family, and at some sketchy motels—wherever God was inviting us to that day.

I learned so much about trust in this adventure because there was no plan. I learned that when your life is 100% up to God to figure out (which by the way, it is, even if you don't live in your car), it's so much easier to be excited for every little thing. So five years ago I began to learn how to be expectant of God, no matter what my situation looked like.

Even now I find myself constantly expecting God to do something amazing. When I'm driving around, I'll just ask God to do something cool and out of the ordinary, just to see. What continues to disappoint me though, is that God doesn't always do the things I want. I tell Jesus, "I believed! I knew that you were capable, and I BELIEVED! So why didn't you do it?" If I'm being honest with you, I still don't have the answer to that question. I know that God is capable of doing big miracles, and I always expect them, but it always seems like God picks another way. Not that God's ways aren't good still, but they just aren't crazy and obvious.

These past few months I've been stuck at my house because of quarantine, and I keep asking God to just make the Coronavirus disappear in a way that would obviously be God. Well, that hasn't been working. And I'm sure God has a plan for that, too. I just wish that sometimes God would do the big thing, even if it isn't necessary.

Maybe you feel like that too. Like you hope and you desire and you dream big! But God never seems to come through. I sometimes wonder if that's how the Israelites felt in Egypt. They knew that God could do miracles; they had seen them done before. In person! Then why would God make them stay in captivity for so long? Then, when God finally freed them from the hands of the Egyptians, they were trapped by the Red Sea. What?!

Do you ever feel like God helps you past one obstacle just for you to turn around and find another one? I've been in a season of roadblocks, and I know how exhausting and frustrating it can be to keep pushing and keep going even when everything seems to be in your way. I also know that we have a Father who wants to help us and be with us when we feel stuck.

People Like Me

Let's go back to the story of the Israelites at the Red Sea. I want you to imagine what they must've been feeling, because maybe you feel this way, too. They were literally trapped between two options: either drown in the Red Sea or be killed by the angry Egyptians. But when the Israelites felt (and were) as trapped as they had ever been, God was going to expand their minds and their perspectives to see the third option, the heavenly option.

Now look at this: verse 13 is where I would absolutely love to be and hate to be Moses at the same time. This is what I feel when I find myself anticipating and expecting God's goodness, but I'm surrounded by people who cannot see the third option. Moses is the one who tells the Israelites that he is expecting God to do something big! Moses sees the third option! Moses got it. He got what God was trying to show them: there is always a third option. But then it gets a little bit awkward. Moses said the thing; Moses believed the thing; but now God asks Moses to do the thing.

God says to Moses, "Why are you crying out to me? Tell the Israelites to move on. Raise your staff and stretch out your hand over the sea to divide the water so that the Israelites can go through the sea on dry ground."

Now is when the trust really kicks in. Let's be honest, if I was in Moses' position here I would not want to raise my staff. Yes, it's a cool idea, but I already said the words. "God, I believed the thing you wanted me to believe, so can you just do the thing now and save us all? I don't want to risk looking weird or foolish in front of the entire group of people that I'm supposed to be leading."

But I think, when you take a step of faith, that's when God will do the thing! And y'all, I know how hard it is. I'm still trying to figure out how to take that one step. Especially in the world we live in with a set-in-stone status quo, it is so hard and so uncomfortable to do some of the things God is calling us to do. The hardest part is when you actually know what God is asking you to do, but you know it's going to take a lot of guts, and you're probably going to get some feedback that you don't like.

Now I invite you to look at Exodus 14: 29-31 (NIV).

> But the Israelites went through the sea on dry ground,
> with a wall of water on their right and on their left.
>
> That day the LORD saved Israel from the hands of the
> Egyptians, and Israel saw the Egyptians lying dead on
> the shore. And when the Israelites saw the mighty
> hand of the LORD displayed against the Egyptians,
> the people feared the LORD and put their trust in him
> and in Moses his servant.

God called Moses to do something risky, with no tangible evidence that it would work. But when Moses did what he was called to do, God was able to use his faith and trust to show the entire tribe of Israelites that God was still in the business of doing big things!

How encouraging is that? God can use even a little bit of faith, faith the size of a mustard seed, to do something miraculous. That means maybe you're like me and you can't take that whole step to do everything you feel called to do. But God is showing me, and maybe God is showing you, too, that even your little tiptoe can make a big difference.

When you feel trusting, you are not alone.

Prayer

God delights in your heart! Jesus loves it when you put your trust in Him, especially in the crazy things! So tell Jesus about the dreams you have and the ways you trust Him in them. Tell God about the ways you wish you trusted more! Use as little or as much of this prayer as you want, and bring your dreams and heart to God.

Hey God!

Thank You so much for the dreams that You've placed on my heart. I ask that You would show me ways to move towards the fulfillment of those dreams as I go through my everyday life. Help me to continue to expect big things from You.

I know that You are a miraculous God who delights in providing for me in glorious ways, so help me to keep my eyes open to Your heavenly actions. Help me to see the third option. I want to see all of the little and big things that You are doing in, around, and through me.

Thank You for helping me to trust You. I ask that You continue to help me trust You in every single aspect of my life.

Thank You for being active in my life. I love You. Amen.

What dreams has God placed on your heart?
Where in your life do you want to trust God more?

Carefree

It's that feeling of such joy. You feel light. You just feel completely free. You don't have a care in the world. You want to smile. You want to sing. You want to dance. Your legs are bouncing and your eyes are shining.

Psalm 150:1-6 (NIV)

"Praise the LORD.
Praise God in his sanctuary;
*   praise him in his mighty heavens.*
Praise him for his acts of power;
*   praise him for his surpassing greatness.*
Praise him with the sounding of the trumpet,
*   praise him with the harp and lyre,*
praise him with timbrel and dancing,
*   praise him with the strings and pipe,*
praise him with the clash of cymbals,
*   praise him with resounding cymbals.*
Let everything that has breath praise the LORD.
Praise the LORD."

Singing in the Shower by Eliana Wiechman

Sometimes you have those days where you just feel so light and happy; that "singing in the shower" kind of feeling. Oftentimes when I feel like this, I turn on some of my favorite music and just sing and dance in front of my mirror. I really don't care what my family thinks of my singing voice or my happiness. I close my eyes and raise my hands. Jump around and dance. Swing on my bed. Fall on the mattress. Sing into my hairbrush. Turn the music up to max volume.

When I feel like this, I don't usually know what made me feel so free and happy. I just am. Maybe you just had an amazing day. Saw a good friend, had a good night's sleep, or maybe you just had that feeling all on its own, with no specific reason why.

When you feel like this, you can invite God to share this awesome feeling with you. Invite God to join you. Thank Jesus for the amazing gift He has given you.

33

In this feeling, praise the Lord. Praise Him with dancing. Praise Him with singing. Praise Him with raised hands and an open heart. Psalm 150 says, *"Praise Him for his acts of power; praise Him for his surpassing greatness."* Praise Him for all He has done for you. Praise the Lord. The Lord who loves you. The Lord who cares for you. Praise Him.

Grab your hairbrush and sing with everything in you! You don't have to care what the people around you think. Just be yourself. Praise the Lord.

People Like Me

In Acts 3, Jesus, through Peter, healed a lame man. The man was so happy, and he rejoiced. He leapt around the temple praising the Lord.

The healed man did not care what others there thought of him. Jesus had given him an amazing gift, and the man praised Him. The lame man danced through the temple. He walked and ran. He sang praises to the Lord. The man who just moments before lay crippled at the front of the temple begging, now danced around praising the Lord.

When you feel carefree, you are not alone.

Let's Pray!

Thank You, God!

Thank You for this amazing gift You have given me, just as the gift You gave the lame man. Thank You for the people You have put in my life. Thank You for the love You show me.

I praise You for Your glory and Your kindness. I praise You for Your love and compassion. I praise You with singing and dancing. I praise You with the sounding of the trumpet. I praise You with the clash of cymbals. I praise You for everything You have ever given me, God.

Amen.

How does your body show joy? What's your favorite way to praise?

Thoughtful

Thoughtfulness can come when you feel calm and relaxed. Lots of times, I am thoughtful after a long day, when my mind is recapping everything that happened. When I am thoughtful, it's like I am exhaling and my body is relaxing into a comfortable position. The external surroundings fade and your thoughts are focused but free.

Philippians 4:8 (NIV)

"Finally, brothers and sisters, whatever is true, whatever is noble, whatever is right, whatever is pure, whatever is lovely, whatever is admirable—if anything is excellent or praiseworthy—think about such things."

Peaceful Thoughtfulness by Kate Rossow

Have you ever fallen asleep in your car? If you have, you know it's not the most comfortable place, but if it's the right time of night and you have had a long day, it can feel like a cloud. In my family when my parents wanted me and my siblings to fall asleep in the car, they would turn on the album *Storm* by Fernando Ortega. Every time it was the same CD. It got to the point that anytime I heard the album, I would automatically get tired and want to go to sleep. (That still happens to this day, by the way.)

I loved when I had an amazing day full of adventure, laughter, and fun with my family and then I got to find this peaceful thoughtfulness at the end of my long day on that car ride home. I got to escape from my busy life, even if it was exciting and good, and go into a time of rest, thankfulness, and thought.

As I fell asleep in the car, I would thank my Lord and think about all the things my God has done for me. I would look out at the stars in the sky and the trees passing by and say what a great God I have. I remember that none of us ever made it to the last song before our heads drooped and we drifted to sleep.

That is a moment in my life that I can pin as feeling a peaceful kind of thoughtfulness or a restful and content kind of feeling. There are, of course, other kinds of thinking. There is stressful thinking, worried thinking, and scary thinking. But this kind of belonging and amazement and joy and peace and love thoughtfulness, that's what I remember feeling on those long car trips home.

Maybe you have an album or song like that. One that brings back feelings where you were at peace thinking about God. Or maybe you feel that way right now, perhaps it's an early morning, you've got your Starbucks in one hand, this book in the other, and you are peacefully, happily being in prayer and thinking about our great God. Maybe it's the other way around where it's a dark, cool night and you are sitting in your bed reading this with your late-night snack in one hand and this book on your lap.

Wherever you are right now, whether you are experiencing a peaceful thoughtfulness, remembering a peaceful thoughtfulness, or looking ahead to when you will feel a peaceful thoughtfulness, I want you to know that Jesus wants to feel that with you. He wants to be present in those experiences and wrap you in His loving arms. If it's the right time of night and you have had a long day, resting in Jesus' arms can feel like a cloud. Jesus wants you to bring Him into your thoughts and wonders.

My dad always says we need to have people "on our rope." He means that we need to have people in our lives who help us throughout our faith walk, people who will pick you up off the ground and help you along. I think Jesus wants to be one of those people, too. He wants to be by your side and in your life just as much as the people you can physically see right now.

So bring Jesus into your peaceful thoughts. Invite Him along on your journey. Share your ideas, worries, dreams, hopes, failures, wonders, and questions with Him. Jesus loves to be part of your thoughtful moments.

People Like Me

In Mark 4, we find a really cool and popular story. It's the story of how Jesus calmed the storm. In verse 35 we see Jesus and his disciples deciding they are going to take a boat ride to the other side of the lake.

Jesus has had a very long day of preaching God's promises and, since He was fully human, He had grown very tired. So He laid down in the stern to take a nap. Jesus was glad to take a quick break from His busy schedule. As He was falling asleep, I imagine Jesus was thinking all kinds of thoughts about His day. Trusting His Father, Jesus was at peace.

When you feel thoughtful, you are not alone.

Prayer

Dear Lord,

In this moment I thank You for all the wonderful things You have done for me. I pray that You would wrap me in Your loving arms and continue to listen to my thoughts and wonders about Your great creation. At this moment I would like to bring those thoughts to Your throne.

Please take some time to tell your Heavenly Father about all the things that have been on your mind recently. You can jot some of them down here:

Lord, I know You hear me and love when I talk to You. Thank You for always being there for me.

Your will be done, Lord.
In Your name I pray, Amen.

Confident

When you feel confident you might notice yourself feeling happier because you are more rooted in who you truly are. You know who you are, and you like that person. You may find yourself feeling less ashamed, but instead, embracing yourself for who you are and how you look. Confidence is that feeling where you feel like you can do pretty much anything. When I feel confident, I'm more likely to stand taller rather than slouch in a corner trying to hide myself.

Galatians 1:15-16 (NIV)

As you read these verses, I encourage you to look and see what parts stand out to you. Ask Jesus to speak to you through this passage and see what He does with it in your heart.

"But when God, who set me apart from my mother's womb and called me by his grace, was pleased to reveal his Son in me so that I might preach him among the Gentiles, my immediate response was not to consult any human being."

Incomparable Beauty by Gabriella Wiechman

Many things in life are more fun when you know more about them. For example, a game is more fun to play when you know the rules, and a party is more fun to attend when you know who you're celebrating. In the same way, I think life is more fun to live when you know who you are.

My entire life I've always known who I was and what God thinks of me. I wasn't always tall, but I always felt like I could conquer the world. One time when I was younger and eating dinner with my family, my dad started talking to all of us. He said, "We are going to ... " and before he could finish his sentence I chimed in with, "TAKE OVER THE WORLD!!!"

I'm not sure if I was joking or serious, because I've always been that way—I've always known that God was on my side and my Heavenly Father created me to be me, so I can do anything! Even when I worry about what I'm going to do with my life, I can always fall back on the confidence that I know who I am in Christ.

I love how Galatians 1 reminds us that we are set apart. God delights in our uniqueness and in the things that make us different. There's a certain peace I feel when I not only know that I am beautiful and capable of amazing things, but when I know that my God thinks those things about me, too.

I love how confident I am, and I love that I love me. Maybe you feel this way, too! You love the parts of your body that not many people like about themselves, and you like the way you laugh and how your eyes sparkle when you smile. You like the way you take charge in a group and help get things done, and you like how you are able to listen when your friend is hurting and needs a shoulder to cry on.

Sometimes being confident can feel selfish, but in this verse Paul says that God is pleased to send Christ into us so that we might stand out and share His gospel. This is such a reassurance because it reminds us that we can live louder and stand taller in the full and certain knowledge that God loves us in our different-ness.

So I encourage you to embrace your confidence in who you are as a child of God and keep living life to the fullest! Continue to love who you are as a unique young woman! And always remember that God loves your uniqueness, so keep it up!

As you embrace who you are, invite Jesus to amplify your confidence through His amazing love for you. Thank the God who made you *you*, and be confident in Christ!

People Like Me

When I think of confident women in the Bible, I immediately think of Esther. She was the definition of a woman who knew who she was and wasn't afraid to do what God called her to do.

She was willing to risk the power and the position she had received from God to do the work God had for her. She stood out in her beauty and her confidence, and she was confident in God to protect her and help her. When you feel confident, you are not alone.

Prayer

God loves to hear from you, and it doesn't sound selfish to your Heavenly Father when you come to Jesus with the things you love about yourself. So feel free to thank God for your good hair days and the days you feel extra beautiful! I promise you God loves to hear you being sure in your identity that is found in Christ.

Hey God!

Thank You so much for making me *me*.

I know some days I don't love every part of me, but right now I'm so thankful that I look like me and act like me.

Thank You for loving me how I am, and for showing me how to love myself like that too.

Thank You for making me uniquely in Your image.

I love You, God! And I love how You made me! Amen.

◆————————————————————————————————◆

While you're feeling really good about yourself, why not make a list of some of the things you like best about how God has made you? That way, when you need a boost, you can check your list and remember some of the things that make you feel confident in who you are in Jesus.

Start your list here:

Anger

Impatient | Irritated | Defensive
Frustrated | Jealous | Prideful

Impatient

Impatience is the emotion that comes from feeling stuck in one place, when you are restlessly eager for something to change or for something new to happen. Frustration and irritability typically accompany this emotion. When I feel impatient, I find myself tapping my fingers or feet or bouncing my knee. I am always looking for something to do to occupy my time. I also find myself thinking about the things I am impatient for, whether that be to leave the house again, see a certain someone, have a test be over, or be a few years into the future.

Acts 1:6-8 (NIV)

"Then they gathered around him and asked him, 'Lord, are you at this time going to restore the kingdom to Israel?'

He said to them: 'It is not for you to know the times or dates the Father has set by his own authority. But you will receive power when the Holy Spirit comes on you; and you will be my witnesses in Jerusalem, and in all Judea and Samaria, and to the ends of the earth.'"

Are We There Yet? by Naomi Rossow

For as long as I can remember, I have felt older than my actual age. With three younger siblings and mostly younger cousins, I am the oldest in most aspects of my family life. This has led to my attitude and behavior (most of the time) reflecting an older age than my actual age. With this comes the tendency to look ahead into the future, specifically, to when my age will match how I feel. When I was a senior in high school, I looked forward to going to college. Now that I am in college, I can't wait until I am in my 20's so I am respected by my peers. I mean, being 18 in high school, you are the oldest there, the most respected and feared. Being 18 in college is like a slap in the face. I found that my opinions and contributions (especially to the dance groups I am a part of) could be overruled by others who have been there longer.

As I interact with people older than me, I ask the question "Are we there yet?" Living through a pandemic, the feeling of impatience comes up in almost every aspect of my life. I see the coronavirus statistics and feel impatient for the numbers to resolve. I drive to my cousins' house and feel impatient for when I can hug my aunt again. I feel a new wave of fear of every person and surface and I feel impatient for some normalcy to return. I complete Spanish class after class and feel impatient to be fluent in the language. I look at my calendar and feel impatient for even the next two weeks of my life to pass.

Throughout my daily life, I ask the question "Are we there yet?"

Looking even further ahead, I see wedding announcements and feel impatient for my own wedding. I have my wedding dress picked out, and I have looked at bridesmaids' dresses. I have my maid of honor picked out. I watch my brother play outside and feel impatient to have kids of my own. Since I can remember, I have wanted to be a mom. My mother is my hero. My aunt is my best friend. I look up to our family friend who has four kids of her own. I am jealous when I see my friends posting pregnancy announcements. I have flash forwards of my own kids when I hold the kids I babysit. These are things that I am not ready for yet, but I am still impatient for them to come.

When I look into the future, I ask the question, "Are we there yet?"

We learn as young Christians that "God has a plan" and "God is in control." These phrases are (1) true and (2) meant to give us a sense of comfort for the sense of uncertainty in our lives.

And they do … sometimes. But I know other times they make me more frustrated. I find it repetitive to hear the phrase "God has a plan" every time I start to feel anxious or impatient. I mean, I know there is a plan, but I don't know what that plan is. And that simple difference can make me more impatient.

Even hearing reassurance, I ask the question, "Are we there yet?"

In Acts 1, right before the Ascension, Jesus addresses the disciples' impatience by reminding them God has a plan, a timeline, they do not know. I imagine they did not like this reminder very much and craved to know what the timeline looked like. But Jesus did not leave it there; He continues to remind them of their position as his disciples. He tells them of the wonderful power of the Holy Spirit who is in them. He affirms them as his witnesses to bring the Word across the world.

As we feel impatient, Jesus invites us to complain to Him. He patiently listens to our concerns knowing that God's timeline is set, and it is good. He is ready to remind us of this fact when we are ready to hear it. But He also is willing to sit and listen. So, tell Him. Complain. Go for it.

And, when you are ready, the reminder of God's timeline will be comforting rather than frustrating. In time, you will hear the reminder that you are sent as ambassadors of the Lord. You will remember your calling as a child of God, your power through the Holy Spirit. But for now, bring your impatience to the Lord. Be frustrated in front of Jesus. He wants to see it. Your Father wants to be present in your heart no matter how it is feeling.

People Like Me

In Numbers 21, the Israelites feel impatient for their destination. They are unhappy with where they are and angry at the LORD (and Moses) for leading them into the desert. They complain to God about their situation saying, "Why have you brought us up out of Egypt to die in the wilderness? There is no bread! There is no water! And we detest this miserable food!" (Numbers 21: 5).

What you are feeling impatient about is probably not that you are wandering around in the wilderness, but the emotion and the response is the same. People all around you feel this way all the time. And this will not be the last time you feel impatient in your life. So, when you get frustrated and antsy, remember: when you feel impatient, you are not alone.

Prayer

Dear Jesus; are we there yet?

I feel like I have reached my potential where I am now. I am ready to move on. I am impatient to take the next step. I know there is a timeline, and I cannot know the details, but Lord, I want to know. I want to be in the loop. I want to be in control. I wish there was something I could do to stop feeling trapped. My impatience to get out of this situation is making me feel more trapped in it. I feel like I am going in circles.

Jesus, I invite You to be present in my impatience. I ask You to ease my fear when the time is right. For now, I am okay being impatient; or at least I am trying to be. Remind me of the blessings I already have. Show me the awe of the moment I am in now. As I look forward to moments that are yet to come, help me to see the moments I am missing by looking ahead. Help me to live in the present.

Be here with me in my impatience, Lord. Amen.

Irritated

Do you ever feel so frustrated, like you just want to hit a tree, or maybe just hide in a corner and cry? In your head, you just keep thinking over and over how everyone—everything—is annoying you. Your teeth may be clenched, your hands in fists, and your heart pumping. Or maybe you're mad at God.

John 11:21 (NIV)

"'Lord,' Martha said to Jesus, 'if you had been here, my brother would not have died.'"

Why, God? by Eliana Wiechman

God, why would you let something like this happen? Many people ask this question. It isn't wrong to think this. It isn't bad. So many things happen that we just don't understand. We don't know why God would let something bad happen to someone good. People may tell you: "God always has a plan," but you just don't see what good could come out of such a thing.

In John 11, I think Martha was irritated with Jesus for being too late. For letting her brother die. She knew that God is good, but she didn't understand why Jesus didn't help when they all knew He could have.

Here's the thing: God did come. Both Mary and Martha seem irritated with Jesus for being late, for not saving their brother. However, Jesus still came, just with a different idea than what they were expecting. Mary and Martha weren't scared to tell Jesus about their disappointment. They knew that He would understand.

God will also understand *your* irritation. God will even come to you, because your story is not yet over, no matter how much it may feel like it.

You will still grieve. You will still hurt. But in spite of all this, know that your story is not yet over. No matter how much you think it is. No matter how much it feels like it. Regardless of the pain you feel, God still loves you. God will make sure that your story doesn't end. God has a way of showing light in even the darkest places.

So, in your irritation remember this and breathe. It is okay to be irritated. It is okay to be angry. It is okay to question and doubt.

Invite Jesus into that brokenness. Place the burden of irritation and blame at his feet. Just like Martha did.

People Like Me

In John 11, Lazarus gets sick. Both of his sisters go to Jesus, but He doesn't get there in time. Lazarus dies. Both Mary and Martha brought their disappointment to Jesus, they told Him that if He would've been there, their brother would not have died.

The two of them were sad. They were irritated. They were irritated with Jesus. They knew He could have helped them, they knew Jesus could have saved their brother, but He didn't.

You may have something like this in your life. You lost a family member. A home. A friend. You had faith that God could have stopped this from happening, but God didn't. In this time of grief and irritation, know that God never left your side. God is not mad at you, even if you're mad at God for letting this happen. You can have peace knowing that God is still there for you. Jesus still loves you. Maybe your loss won't be undone until the New Creation, but God still has a way of making things better, even now. When you feel irritated, you are not alone.

Let's Pray!

Dear God,

I need Your help. I've lost something and I'm mad. I know that You could have stopped this from happening, but You didn't. I don't understand how You could let something like this happen.

God, I know You have a plan, but knowing that doesn't make me feel any better. Please help me. Show me that You love me. That You are still with me and You are still a good God even in the hard times.

Jesus, I invite You into my anger and irritation; I blame You for the change in my life. I wish You would have stopped it or changed the outcome. I am irritated with You right now. So, come to me in my irritation because I am not ready to stop being irritated with You yet.

Please come to me. Help me accept You. Help me to know that my story is not over. Even when I am in such a place of darkness, please, be a light to guide me. Amen.

Defensive

This emotion surfaces when you feel threatened by someone or something. It closes you off to the people and things around you in an attempt to keep you safe. When I am feeling defensive, I tend to snap at people in a conversation quicker than normal. I find myself sitting away from the action where I would normally be in the middle of it. My RBF face comes out ... or in other words, I sit with a scowl on my face rather than a smile or content expression.

Exodus 14:4 (NIV)

"The LORD will fight for you; you need only to be still."

Authority and Blame by Naomi Rossow

Bees only sting if they feel under attack or their hive is threatened. We're like that, too: when we feel attacked, our first, primitive instinct is to defend ourselves. If someone jumps on your back and you perceive it as a physical threat, you try to fling them off and protect yourself.

This defensive instinct applies to our relationships and emotions as well. Some of the most common triggers for my defense mechanism are threats to my authority and attacks that seem to blame. But I don't always need a reason to feel defensive...

Let's look at attacks on authority first. Think of someone you have authority over. Maybe a younger sibling you watch when your parents go away. Maybe kids you babysit. Maybe some kids in the grade below you. Maybe you are on the board of a club and have authority over other people in the club.

That last one is true for me. I have authority in my position on the board of a dance club at my college. I absolutely love the dance group and I love being able to help run it and make sure everyone is comfortable. But I was only 18 when I was given a board position. At the time I had only been part of the club for less than one semester. Because I was still relatively new to the group and I was younger than everyone there, my authority got overruled a lot by other people.

Now, I am a person who appreciates and respects hierarchy, so even if I don't agree with the person in charge of me, I follow their lead because they are above me in the chain of command. In the same way, when people don't respect my authority, I get upset and defensive.

You may not feel the same way about hierarchy as I do. Your defensive nature might be sparked by wanting to be right or wanting things to be done your way. When people second-guess your knowledge or experience, that can also feel like an attack on your personal authority.

People also tend to get defensive when they feel like they are being blamed for something (whether or not they are guilty). Think of a time when you made a mistake. Even though you knew you were at fault, you still probably got defensive when someone else blamed you.

Even when you are guilty, your instinct is still to defend and protect yourself. But you get even more defensive when you are being blamed for something you did not do. Imagine if your sibling or friend broke your mom's favorite vase. If your mom punishes you for something you didn't do, you most likely would not sit back and allow it. Your natural instinct is to protect yourself. (I know I would be more likely to take the fall for my friend than for my sibling. What would you do?)

There are even times when you feel defensive for no apparent reason. Maybe it has just been a long day and you are snippy at everyone. Maybe you are overtired because you have been doing a lot of fun things and you have reached your limit. Maybe you have had one thing after another that upsets you, and this is the final straw. Or maybe you are on your period and everyone seems like they are provoking you.

Everyone gets defensive. When we get defensive, we tend to do one of two things: pick fights or push the feeling down. If you call names, someone else gets hurt. If you push it down, the feelings of anger or aggression can eventually come out even stronger.

So next time you are feeling defensive, try inviting Jesus into your defensive feelings and be defensive with Him. You don't have to hold back. It's okay. You're not perfect. So don't try to be. Just like every other emotion, allow yourself to feel what you are feeling; but feel it with Jesus. Tell Him what makes you feel like you are under attack. Tell Him who deserves to get it, and why. Ask Jesus how He is defending you or what you should do with the blame you feel. Even if you don't have a good reason for your feelings, Jesus is ready to listen. He's good at that.

People Like Me

In Acts 5, Peter and the Apostles are preaching in the temple courts after escaping from jail. When confronted by the Pharisees, they do not back down and stop preaching. Instead, Peter says, "We must obey God rather than other human beings" (Acts 5:29). Naturally, this sparks anger and defensiveness in the Pharisees, and they even want to have the Apostles killed.

Then this Pharisee named Gamaliel steps forward to talk. Gamaliel uses God's power and ultimate control over history to convince the other Pharisees to consider more carefully what they will do to the Apostles. He says, "Leave these men alone! Let them go! For if their purpose or activity is of human origin, it will fail. But if it is from God, you will not be able to stop these men; you will only find yourselves fighting against God" (Acts 5:38-39).

Gamaliel steps calmly into the middle of an angry and stubborn confrontation between the Apostles and Pharisees and uses God's name to foster peace. When you are feeling defensive, you can want to have a stand-off with another person. But maybe Jesus is inviting you to let Him be your defender and let Him take care of it.

When you feel defensive, you are not alone.

Prayer

Hey Jesus,

I really don't want to talk right now. I am super defensive toward the people I love. I am closed off to them and fighting them on every little thing.

This is me inviting You into my defensiveness. I am trying to open myself up to You even though I feel closed off to everyone. Lord, please send Your Spirit into me and into this moment.

Okay; bye for now.

Frustrated

When I'm frustrated, I get mad at all of the small things that someone does wrong. You can lose your temper a lot while you are experiencing frustration. You might feel your body tense up and your temperature rise.

Isaiah 41:10 (ESV)

"Fear not for I am with you;
be not dismayed, for I am your God;
I will strengthen you, I will help you,
I will uphold you in my righteous right hand."

Ahhhhhh! by Kate Rossow

Feeling frustrated is something that comes and goes. One moment you could be mad at your siblings and the next minute hugging them. You could be frustrated with yourself, frustrated with others, or even frustrated with God.

First, being frustrated with yourself can happen when you get a bad grade on your math test and you are mad at yourself for not studying hard enough. Or you could be frustrated with yourself if you and your friend are in an argument because of something you did. This frustration typically manifests itself through yelling or crying or maybe even punching walls.

Guilt is probably associated with this type of frustration as well. I remember a time when I felt so frustrated at myself because I had gotten nothing done during the day and so I wanted to throw my phone and yell and just fight myself.

Second, you can also be frustrated at other people. If your brother doesn't stop yelling after you ask him to, you could be frustrated at him. Or if your mom tells you to get off your phone and go outside, you could become frustrated at your mom for always telling you what to do.

This frustration typically manifests itself in the form of harsh words, snapped responses, and even physical retaliation. I get frustrated at my little brother a lot because he just continues to make weird noises in my face, whining, and overall being an annoying little brother. When this happens, I usually start snapping at him and rolling my eyes while trying not to yell. It can be hard to keep myself in check during these times because I am so frustrated.

Finally, you can also be frustrated with God. If your life is going bad you could start being frustrated at your Heavenly Father. I know from past experience how it feels when everything in your life changes in the blink of an eye. It's happened to me multiple times.

It's okay to be frustrated with Jesus. Don't try to hide it from Him. Jesus knows everything, every thought, emotion, word, deed, but He wants you to bring them to Him. You can't hide anything, including emotions, from Jesus because He knew you were going to get frustrated at Him before you were even born. So just talk to Him about what is frustrating you. Knowing that God knows everything can be intimidating, but remember God *wants* you to bring *all* your emotions to the cross.

Now, go back up and read Isaiah 41:10 again. What did you notice differently this time? No matter who you are frustrated with, God promises to be with you always.

In Isaiah, God tells us that we can count on the help and strength of God. Your Heavenly Father is never going to leave you even if you are frustrated at yourself, others, or even God. In fact, your Savior is upholding you with his righteous right hand, strengthening you, and helping you, every step of the way. Including the frustrating ones.

People Like Me

In Exodus and Numbers, while the Israelites are roaming through the wilderness, they complain a lot. In Exodus chapter 16, they are complaining about the quail and manna the Lord was sending them. They even went as far as to say that they wished they were back in slavery in Egypt because at least there they had pots of meat and enough bread to fill their bellies.

That sounds to me like extreme frustration at Moses, Aaron, and God. They were so frustrated that they didn't have meat and bread that they wished to go back to a place of torture and enslavement. God didn't give up on those frustrated, frustrating people. And God won't give up on you. When you feel frustrated, you are not alone.

Prayer

Invite God into your heart as you struggle with your frustration.

Dear Jesus,

Thank You for always being around me and holding me. Please help me know that being frustrated is just part of life, and I can bring You into my frustration. Thanks for not giving up on me!

Your will be done, Lord.

In Your name I pray, Amen.

Capture Your Emotions Faith Experiment

In my experiences of being frustrated at someone, I am sometimes covering up another emotion, such as sadness or jealousy.

Take some time to talk to Jesus and go in depth about what or who you are frustrated with. He might open your eyes to see that you are actually jealous of someone or something they have, which makes you frustrated that you can't have it. Or you could be sad or experiencing grief, and instead of embracing that sadness, you are pushing it away and getting frustrated at everyone you come in contact with.

Google an Emotion Wheel, or use the one on the front cover of this book, to try and put a label on the emotion you are covering up with frustration. As you pray, use the space below to write down emotion words that stick out to you and help capture how you're feeling.

Jealousy can be a subtle emotion that shows up in offhand thoughts and small actions. Regardless, jealousy can be a powerful emotion. When you are jealous, you may find yourself thinking of the person or thing you are jealous of more often than normal. These thoughts can be unkind or maybe even violent. You plot a way to get what you want. Your daily actions may change to match your new thoughts. When I am jealous, I find that I am in the corner of the room rather than the center. I stand in a more slouched position with slit eyes, like the villain in a movie.

Proverbs 27:4 (NIV)

"Anger is cruel and fury overwhelming, but who can stand before jealousy?"

Wicked Witch of the West by Naomi Rossow

Movie villains take many forms and have many motives, but one of the most common is jealousy. Anger is hot and intense; jealousy is calm and slow.

One of the most notable times I have felt jealous was in middle school and high school. I was jealous of my best friend because I thought she was prettier than me. She always had better clothes than I did. Her makeup was better than mine. Her notebooks in school were fancier. She had a boyfriend before I did. Her family owned an RV and went camping together. She got her driver's license before I did. Her dad bought her a car. She was a dancer. She was a part of the group I saw as "the cool kids." I was jealous of all these things through both middle and high school.

My jealousy led me to change who I was and how I acted. My clothing style changed to be more similar to hers. I started wearing makeup. And then more makeup... I took hair tips from her to make my hair just a little bit better. The words I used and the cadence I spoke in changed slightly. And all of these changes were minute. They took time and were subconscious. They were my jealousy taking physical action.

As time passed, my jealousy faded more and more. I became more confident in myself and my looks. I started to personalize the things I had taken from her. My jealousy was not aggressive enough to cause real issues in my life. However, I know jealousy can be devastating.

As you struggle with the subtle yet real feeling of jealousy, bring it to the Lord. As your Friend, Jesus wants to hear about your problems. Your Heavenly Father wants to hear about your struggles. God, the Creator of the universe, delights in you. Invite Jesus into your jealousy. Don't try and change what you are feeling to do so. Just pray the simple prayer, "Come, Holy Spirit." Ask God what's going on in your life right now. See Jesus in the subtle cadences of your life.

People Like Me

The book of Genesis is most famous for the account of creation. But there are so many other important stories. One of these is the story of *Joseph and the Amazing Technicolor Dreamcoat*. You know; like the musical.

Joseph had ten older half-brothers who didn't like him very much. Or really at all. Maybe because Joseph was kind of a snobby little brat, a real daddy's boy. The brothers were so jealous of Joseph that they sold him to a passing Egyptian slave-trader. Imagine being so jealous of your little brother that you sold him on eBay, and then told your father he was killed by wild animals!

The good news is that God had a plan for Joseph. And his brothers. Years later, when there was a famine in the land, Joseph's brothers traveled to Egypt for food. When they arrived, guess who was in charge of food distribution? Joseph!

Joseph's brothers got a second chance. Eventually, Joseph was able to forgive them. Joseph learned that even when we intend something for evil, God can intend it for good. Jealousy is not the end of the story. God forgives you and gives you a second (and third) chance.

When you feel jealous, you are not alone.

Prayer

Come, Holy Spirit,

Join me in my jealousy. I do not like feeling this way. And I don't know how to control it. Sometimes my jealous feelings are prominent in my life and other times I forget my jealousy is there.

God, what are You working in my life right now? Open my eyes to You and work through this jealousy. Amen.

Prideful

Feeling prideful is feeling better than everyone else. You may begin to think that others' failures are your victories and that your own victories are more important than other people. You may walk with your head held higher and with a puffed-out chest. Some emotions that often go along with pride are jealousy, greed, and false confidence.

Proverbs 16:18-19 (NIV)

"Pride goes before destruction,
a haughty spirit before a fall.

Better to be lowly in spirit along with the oppressed
than to share plunder with the proud."

Pride Before the Fall by Liz Rossow

Pride is one emotion in the Bible that is expressly condemned. Over and over the Scriptures tell us that the proud will be humbled or that the Lord despises the proud. When the Bible talks about pride in this way, it is referring to the jealous pride that comes from feeling like you are better than everyone, like you deserve more or are on the next level. This type of pride isolates you from others and from God.

This self-centered pride destroys relationships. If you believe that you are better than they are, how could you have a real relationship with another person?

Pride is an emotion or character trait often associated with the villain in a story. They are too high and mighty to accept help or see the damage they do to others. The hero understands humility and the need to have companions. This is what allows the hero to prevail over the villain. Pride comes before the villain's fall.

So why do we still fall victim to it? If the Bible condemns it, if it destroys relationships, and if all of our stories warn against it, why do we still fall into this trap?

Our own sinful nature works to morph our God-given successes and victories into tools to turn us away from God. Your sinful ego wants you to think that all of your victories are solely your own, without God. We naturally want independence from other people, and even from God.

Pride does not even have to come after a victory: it may come after someone else's failure. If Susan trips over her shoes, you may think, "Wow I would never be that clumsy." That's pride. The phrase, "I would never," places yourself higher than someone else. That's sinful pride. You may even place yourself above God. Have you ever thought, maybe after an achievement, "I did it all by myself?" Discrediting other people in your achievements can all too easily become your pride placing yourself above others, and even above God.

This pride—the jealous, angry, mean pride—is the pride that the Bíble condemns. This pride not an easy pattern to break. Because we live in a sinful world, our sinful nature wants us to put ourselves first. Thankfully, we don't have to fight this battle alone. Jesus came and laid down His life for us in an ultimate act of humility so that we are able to turn to Him when we feel sinfully proud.

Jesus grants us forgiveness, and He also gives us a place to wrestle with the idea of humility. As you place yourself above others, invite Jesus to come to you and help you walk in humility. Jesus knows the temptation of pride and will help you walk through it.

People Like Me

The devil manipulated pride in the Garden of Eden. He told Eve that if she ate the fruit that God had forbidden, she would be like God, all-knowing. And I mean, you know, girls: we often like to be in control and know the plan. So, Eve in her pride wanted to be all-knowing. She did not want to be beneath God. So she ate the fruit. That's sinful pride.

Satan took the good humility that was in the world and that was in Eve and turned it into pride that destroyed God's creation. This is the first and ultimate example of "Pride goes before The Fall."

But God didn't leave Eve on her own in her pride. Though Eve and Adam were exiled from the Garden, God promised to go with them, and to send a savior. In the same way when you feel pride, even sinful pride, you are not alone.

Prayer

Dear Jesus,

Help me overcome this pride I feel. Help me to see my victories as Your victories rather than from my own power. Even when I achieve the goal I have been working for, humble my heart, and help me give You the glory.

Enter my prideful heart and give me humility. Help me put others before myself, and You above all.

And, Jesus, when I don't succeed at these things, when I fail to give You the glory, when I find confidence in other people's failures, come to me in my pride. Do not abandon me. Guide me once again to Your path of humility. Help me, Lord. Amen.

———

Pride is a tricky emotion. Is your pride healthy, or sinful? Because you are a mixed person, your pride is probably also mixed.
Below, write down some things you are proud of. Then invite Jesus to look at those feelings with you. Where you can see gloating or arrogance or sin, ask Jesus to take that away. Where you have confidence and gratefulness and a sense of achievement, take a moment to say thanks.

Joy

Proud | Triumphant | Celebration
Grateful | Awestruck | Delight

Proud

You may walk taller when you feel pride. You will want to tell everyone about the event, action, thing, or person you are proud of. You may feel happy satisfaction. Smiling is often associated with this version of the emotion.

Matthew 3:17 (NIV)

"And a voice from heaven said, 'This is my Son, whom I love; with him, I am well pleased.'"

Ephesians 2:8-9 (ESV)

"For by grace you have been saved through faith. And this is not your own doing; it is the gift of God, not a result of works, so that no one may boast."

Well Pleased by Liz Rossow

What do you think about when you think of being proud of something, or of someone being proud of you? I think about when my dad tells me he is proud of me for finishing a hard school year or doing well in a theatre performance. I think about the pride I feel when my friends accomplish something they had been working hard toward, or the pride I feel when I get a good grade on a test.

I wanted to talk about the joy pride brings and how we can glorify God through our pride, but when I went looking for a Bible verse to accompany this devotion, all I found was damnation. If you google what the Bible says about pride you will get results that, summed up, mean if you are proud you are going to hell. That was a real self-esteem killer.

I then had to figure out, if I was proud that I got a good grade, did that mean that I was disgracing God or making God angry? That did not feel right. By feeling good about something I did I was not putting myself in the place of God or saying that I did not need God, was I?

The society I live in has modified the meaning of "pride." The proud feeling I'm thinking of is better defined as "well pleased." When you do a good job on a test, you are "well pleased" with yourself. Instead of your dad saying that he is proud of you, he could say, "I am well pleased with you." This is not the same as putting yourself above God or acting like you don't need God.

Jesus loves you for who you are. That extends to the good test grade or great performance. He gives you those talents and victories. You do not need to hide a victory given to you by God; just treat it as a gift from your Heavenly Father. If "well pleased" starts turning into a prideful attitude that replaces God, you have an issue. But the feeling of being "well pleased" with yourself or with others is a gift given by God to us so that we are able to see God's goodness and love.

The next time you succeed or feel "well pleased" with yourself, give glory to God, the God of Joy and Victory. Invite Jesus into your joyful pride and look for what He is working in your heart.

People Like Me

When Jesus was baptized, God spoke. The Father opened the heavens and said, "This is my Son, whom I love; with him, I am well pleased." God the Father was well pleased. God was proud of Jesus. Jesus was doing good work in the name of the Father which resulted in the Father declaring pride in Jesus. This is not a self-righteous or sinful pride. It is taking pleasure in the good work of others for God's will and purpose.

When you feel proud, when you feel well pleased, you are not alone.

Prayer

Dear Heavenly Father,

Thank You for the gifts and talents You give to me. Thank You for the wonderful people You have surrounded me with, and for their amazing accomplishments. Help me to use the gifts You give to glorify Your name above all others.

I am proud of who I am right now.

And I am proud of who I am in You.

All the glory to You forever and ever, Amen.

Triumphant

When I feel triumphant, I am usually very proud of something I have done. My cheeks get red and sometimes I cry happy tears if it was an especially huge success. I sense a huge weight getting taken off my shoulders, and my heart feels very light. I feel as though I could fly.

2 Samuel 6:5 (NIV)

"David and all Israel were celebrating with all their might before the LORD."

Feeling Triumphant with God by Kate Rossow

I play a lot of sports, like basketball, cheerleading, volleyball, and track. One thing all sports have in common is that everyone is playing to win, whether that be beating your personal record or winning against another person or group of people. When people win, they feel triumphant.

There are a few times when I felt triumphant in sports that really stick out in my memory. The first was when I made states in fourth grade for track and winning eighth place. Then, two years later, I made the varsity team in basketball and we made it to states the next year.

Maybe you play sports and can connect to what I'm saying or maybe you can think of another time when you felt triumphant. Perhaps you got the part in the show you wanted or baked a really cool cake. Or maybe you feel triumphant after you finish a series on Netflix. (I certainly do.)

Your Heavenly Father wants to celebrate in your triumphs and victories with you. Sometimes when I am feeling triumphant I imagine Jesus dancing next to me and telling me good job. It's just a way for me to feel Him near me.

And it's not just that you imagine Jesus there, He *is* there! God is there in your triumph and victories every time. Your Father loves to see you happy. Jesus loves to see you smile and feel good about something you have accomplished. He loves it. So invite our Savior and friend into your heart so you can experience triumph *with* your Heavenly Father. Jesus is working through your triumph and wants to be triumphant with you!

People Like Me

David, one of the Bible's greatest heroes, experienced a lot of triumph in his life. The story he is best known for is his fight with Goliath in 1 Samuel. The Bible says, *"David triumphed over the Philistine with a sling and a stone."*

Of course, when we think of David, we think King David. But you have to remember at this point in his life he was the youngest son of a shepherd. He was a nobody, and yet he had the courage and strength and trust in God to defeat this giant Philistine. That's crazy. Can you imagine the bragging rights he had over his brothers after that?

And after David killed the giant, I can't even imagine how loud the battle cry would have been from all of the Israelite soldiers before they drove out the opposing army and plundered their camp. I imagine their cry would have shaken the ground at their feet. And you know God was getting all the glory! I bet God's shouts of triumph were even louder!

Later, when David became king, he celebrated another victory. As they brought the Ark of the Covenant into his capital city, King David danced his heart out in the presence of the LORD!

I'll let that image sink into your brain for a minute. Now, join me in a dance party with Jesus to celebrate your success! When you feel triumphant, you are not alone.

Prayer

Dear Jesus,

Thank You for all the moments of triumph You have given me over the years. I ask that You would bless me with many more in the future. Thank You that You love to see me happy and celebrating, and that You are right there celebrating and dancing with me.

Please help me not become too prideful, but help me serve and honor You throughout all that I accomplish and do. And let's get this party on!

Your will be done, Lord.

In Your name I pray, Amen.

Celebration

A graduation, baby shower, wedding, birthday, or just seeing your friends again for the first time in a while: celebration is a happy emotion that makes you feel light inside. When I am in a celebratory mood, my chest lifts, and I walk light on my feet. I might even bounce or run rather than walk. I have a lot more energy because I am excited about the celebration.

Psalm 101:11 (NIV)

"I will sing of your love and justice; to you, LORD, I will sing praise."

A Time of Celebration by Naomi Rossow

In my family, we have a special birthday tickle song we sing each year. We are only allowed to sing this song once, so it has to be sung with as much of the family as possible. It goes as follows:

> *Come children and join in our festival song,*
> *And hail the sweet joy which this day brings along!*
> *We will join our glad voices in one hymn of praise*
> *To God who has kept us and lengthened our days.*
>
> *Happy birthday to you! Happy birthday to you!*
> *Happy birthday dear ___; Happy birthday to YOU!*

During the "Happy Birthday" stanza of that song, the birthday person is tickled on each "you." Now, over the years, the idea of tickling only on the "you" has gotten lost in translation. It's a lot more common to be tickled throughout the whole birthday stanza. This song is a sign of celebration in my family. Smiles are shared and laughter fills the house.

Celebrations take many forms: birthday parties, memorials, holidays, anniversaries, etc. Each of these is celebrated in a different way. You may have had a princess-themed birthday party as a young girl. Or your parents may have had a wedding anniversary with adult friends and champagne. Maybe you celebrated a big sports win with your friends at a restaurant, or the opening night for your big performance with flowers.

Or maybe you celebrate a family tradition on July 4th or Christmas Eve. There are endless reasons you may be celebrating right now, and even more ways to celebrate them.

When we celebrate, we are celebrating gifts from God. We praise God for the things we've been given and invite God into our celebrations. Take a moment in the excitement and celebration to say a silent, loud, formal, or casual "thank You" to your Heavenly Father.

People Like Me

The Parable of the Lost Son in Luke 15 is a relatively well-known story. Jesus tells of a man who had two sons. One of these sons took his share of the inheritance and left home. After spending all the money and running his reputation into the ground, he returned home in shame, hoping his father would let him become a servant of the house so that he may have food to eat and a place to sleep.

When his father saw him in the distance, the son was greeted with joyful shouts and tears of relief. To celebrate the return of his son, the father ordered the prize calf to be killed for a feast. There was music and dancing as the whole house celebrated the lost son's return.

Although we may not order our finest calf to be slaughtered, events and people are celebrated around the world in a countless number of ways. We celebrate with traditional music and dance, as well as not-so-traditional music and dance. Joyous tears are shared between friends and family. Your celebration is shared by those in the room with you who cherish the same person or event that sparked the celebration. Your God is also there celebrating, singing, and dancing with you. When you are celebrating, you are not alone.

Prayer

I can't contain my joy. Lord, You have blessed me greatly.

Today, I celebrated with the people closest to me. We laughed. We danced. We talked. We smiled. Thank You for these people. Thank You for this day. Come into my celebration as I praise You in each giggle and each head bob. Use Your Spirit to shine through my beaming face.

Lord, You are good. Thank You.

Grateful

When you are grateful you might feel a calm, satisfying feeling in your chest. You feel complete and full. You might notice yourself worrying less about the little things and choosing to focus instead on what makes your heart happy.

Psalm 136:1 (NIV)

"Give thanks to the LORD, for he is good. His love endures forever."

Grateful for the Little Things by Gabriella Wiechman

A few years ago, I went on my first mission trip. By the time I came home, my entire perspective had changed.

A group of women from my friends' church in Michigan invited my mom on their trip to Uganda. My mom invited me to go with her, which at the time made absolutely no sense because I was terrified of everything, but looking back, I think it's how the Spirit planted a desire in my heart to serve God's people in other countries. A few weeks later I was on a plane with my mom on our way to Africa.

I don't remember much from that trip, but what I do remember was seeing extreme poverty and a lack of physical possessions, and wondering how someone could live like that. I wonder even now how someone could keep their pride when they were sleeping in a house literally made of dirt and straw.

But that's not the only thing I remember from my short time in Uganda. What sticks in my mind more than the poverty these people lived in is the smiles they had on their faces. I can still picture the women and children dancing around, singing, and screaming out of joy. Not some fabricated joy that comes from a toy or a nice paycheck. No. This was the realest joy I've ever seen in my life.

It wasn't just the smiles on their faces; it was the joy overflowing from their hearts. That was the hottest, stickiest, dustiest day ever, but no one was bothered by the heat. We were all dancing, covered in sweat and red dirt, screaming at the tops of our lungs. I remember being so awestruck by the joy and gratitude each woman had, even in the absence of electricity, air conditioning, and clean water.

It didn't take me long to realize that the reason these women didn't hang their heads in shame is because they didn't find their pride in material things; they actually found their pride in Jesus Christ. Every ounce of joy they possessed came straight from God. There was no need to have a mansion overflowing with designer shoes and fancy dresses; they found their worth in God.

Last October, I had the opportunity to go on another mission trip, this time to El Salvador. Once again I was in awe of how blessed the people I met were. They were so proud of their community and their families instead of their houses and cars, and I loved that. Sometimes, when I think about these communities I was welcomed into, I find myself being more and more grateful for things that really matter.

When I begin to think about all the ways God has blessed me, it can be overwhelming. I don't always realize how blessed I am to have my own room, my own car, my own job, etc. These things that I so often find myself complaining about are things that some people have been praying for. So when I think about how grateful these people who had practically nothing were, it inspires me to notice God's provision in my daily life, and I want to invite you to do that, too.

Psalm 136 thanks God for everything, blessings big and small, from the sun giving us light, to the parting of the Red Sea and saving the Israelites. These words teach us to be grateful in every situation, and that in every situation, God's love endures.

I think a major part of feeling truly grateful is trusting that God will provide for your needs. When you trust that God has a plan and that God will provide everything you need, then it's easier to feel grateful for anything extra God chooses to bless you with. When you go through life not expecting anything, but instead simply receiving what God has to give you, it makes life so much more beautiful. If you decide to be satisfied with knowing God and having Jesus in your life, then even your family becomes a bigger blessing.

Although it sounds really nice to "simply receive what God has for you," in reality it's one of the hardest things to do, especially in our materialistic culture. When everything and everyone around you is telling you to do more and get more, it's a lot harder to focus on what God is doing and what Jesus is trying to give you.

So as I'm learning to be grateful for every little thing, I'm also trying to invite God into where I am right now. I still miss things and forget to thank God for all sorts of blessings, but God still loves me. I don't always notice the blessings Jesus gives me, but my Jesus still delights in showering me with His goodness and love.

As I am growing in my gratefulness, though, I have noticed some really amazing things that before I would have just walked right by. I've learned to change my perspective in order to witness the amazing things God has been doing all along! But my greatest comfort is that God continues to flood my life with blessings no matter how many of them I notice, and as I continue to grow in my relationship with Christ, my eyes are opened to see and receive all of His beautiful gifts for me.

People Like Me

Paul wrote about some people I wish I knew. They were from a place called Macedonia, and Paul brags about them. He says, "In the midst of a very severe trial, their overflowing joy and their extreme poverty welled up in rich generosity" (2 Corinthians 8:2, NIV). Isn't that amazing? Overflowing joy and extreme poverty can go together! The people in Macedonia experienced that; the people I met in Uganda and El Salvador experienced that. I sometimes catch a glimpse of that, too. Your joy doesn't come from your stuff. What a relief!

When you feel grateful, you are not alone.

Prayer

Hey God,

Thank You so much for all of the things that You've blessed me with throughout my life. Thank You for my family and my house. Thank You for giving me food to eat. But most importantly, thank You for being my friend. Thank You for the way that You love me and take care of me, even when it's hard to see or if it doesn't make sense to me.

God, I ask that You would help me change the way I view things; help me see the beauty that You see. Help me to notice the many blessings You put in my life. Would You please give me opportunities to be grateful and a place to express my praise for the ways You are at work in my life? Thank You for all that You have done and continue to do for me.

I love You, God. Amen.

Faith Experiment: Noticing God This Week

For the next five days, write down at least one thing that made you notice God. Maybe a Bible verse popped up on your social media feed that really hit home. Maybe the Starbucks barista said something kind to you at the beginning of your day. Maybe one of your friends texted you out of the blue to tell you how thankful they are to have you in their life. Or maybe there's a day where the only thing you could find to be grateful for was a pretty sunrise or your bed, and that's okay! Sometimes the Spirit wants to show Jesus to you through the little things, too.

No matter how or where God shows up, the Spirit invites you to look for God and invite Jesus into every part of your life, with no shame or guilt!

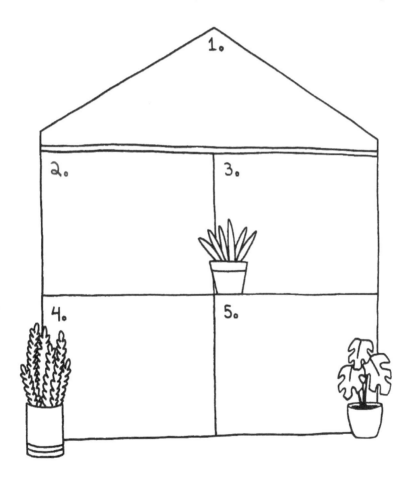

Awestruck

Awestruck is amazement at all God has done. When your head feels like it's going to explode because of how great our God is, you are awestruck. You may feel tiny and useless because of how huge and powerful God is. You may just feel thankful that you get to be living in God's creation and breathing the air that God gave you. You may not know exactly what to think or do, like the breath was knocked out of you ... but in a good way. There is probably a smile on your face as you stand in the face of something you don't fully understand.

2 Samuel 7:22 (NIV)

"How great you are, Sovereign LORD! There is no one like you, and there is no God but you, as we have heard with our own ears."

How Great Is Our God by Kate Rossow

When you think of God, do you think of how great and amazing the creation is? Do you think of the way that God wove the fabric of the world together by speaking? I do. Our God is so great.

When I am sitting in the car driving to school or to the grocery store or to church, I usually look out the window and see our Father's creation. It amazes me every time. I mean, the detail in the brown, hard bark on every tree! The brilliance behind the big fluffy white things above my head and the beautiful blue blanket that is draped over my head!

Every night before I close my blinds and go to sleep, I look out my window and see the specks of light hovering above me and the still water of the lake below. I look at the round light hanging from an invisible string and think about how creative our Father is.

Our God is so good. God has unconditional love for us: unbelievable, outstanding, perfect, never-ending, beautiful love!

So what do we do when we feel like bursting because of how great our God is? Praise your Savior. Praise Jesus for all He has done. Thank Him for the life that He has given you. Let yourself burst.

Psalm 96:1 (ESV) says, *"Oh sing to the LORD a new song; sing to the LORD, all the earth!"* Sing your praises. It's okay if you're not the best singer. Jesus won't care. Sing to the Lord!

70

People Like Me

A few days ago I saw a rainbow stretched across a lake. It reminded me of the promise that God made to Noah when the very first rainbow appeared in the sky.

Can you imagine walking out of an ark that you had started building a year ago in a desert, having two of each animal behind you, having just seen everybody drown by the waters overflowing from the sky and the ground and then seeing the very first rainbow? If I were Noah, I would be pretty awestruck looking back at my life.

Even though we don't see God work in the same way Noah did, we do see God's amazing works of mercy, just in different ways. How do you see God working in your life today? Just like Noah, when we see God's wonderful hand at work in our lives, we can feel awestruck.

When you feel awestruck, you are not alone.

Prayer

Dear Lord,

You are so powerful and mighty. You are the greatest artist and creator I know. Thank You that You chose to love me unconditionally and always be there for me. You truly are great, Lord.

Your will be done, Lord. In Your name I pray, Amen.

What's one place in the world where you have experienced awe in creation?
Write some details you remember below or paste a picture here.

Delight

Delight is a feeling of extreme happiness. Smiling, laughing, jumping, and spinning may occur. A *Whoo-hoo!* feeling all over your body is one possible side effect. Things that commonly cause delight are personal success, a friend's success, good news, or fulfilment of a wish.

Hebrews 12:2 (NIV)

"Looking to Jesus, the founder and perfecter of our faith, who for the joy that was set before him endured the cross, despising the shame, and is seated at the right hand of the throne of God."

Delightful Joy by Liz Rossow

Delight. Doesn't that word just want to make you smile? I love that word. I love that feeling, the ecstatic exclamation of joy so overwhelming you don't know what to do with it. To me, this word is the feeling of smiling so much your cheeks hurt, and not in the bad fake-smile kind of way. Delight makes me want to jump up and down and laugh because it is so wonderful.

I am known as a happy person. I am the resident happy person in my friend groups. Smiles, optimism, and upbeat energy is kind of my thing. Being happy is great, but it is nothing compared to delight. Happiness can be manufactured. It can be stretched to cover way too much, or it can be gone in a flash. Delight is the big leagues.

Think of your happiest memory. Did you just smile? I bet you were delighted in that memory and you feel delight just thinking of it. Some movies have montages of characters being happy or feeling delight. Normally these are before the main conflict when the two main love interests get together in a teen rom-com, but it does not have to be romantic. Think back on your life. What moments would be added in your *delight montage?* Don't just think of the big moments like a first kiss or the birth of a sibling, but think of all the little moments: winning a game of cards, eating ice cream with a friend, each hug from your favorite person.

Those are moments God sees and wants to be a part of. God wants to live in your delight because God delights in you. That cumulative feeling of pure delight that all of those big and small memories bring is what Jesus feels every time He thinks of you.

In your delight, pray and ask God to come and rejoice with you. You are a unique individual whom God absolutely delights in; your Heavenly Father wants to share that delight with you in whatever causes you to delight.

People Like Me

Consider Psalm 18. In the first part of Psalm 18, David talks about how he was in great danger and called out to the LORD for help, for salvation. David writes how the LORD shook the earth in anger and came down in smoke and fire with cherubim and bolts of lightning. God came roaring out of the heavens to come to David's rescue. Why? David puts it this way: "The LORD rescued me, *because he delighted in me.*"

God delights in you. The feeling of jumping up and down because you can't contain your joy is what the Lord of heaven and earth feels about you. When you feel delighted, you are not alone.

Prayer

Everything I have to delight in comes from You, so thank You, Lord!

Thank You, Jesus, for going to the cross because You delighted in me. Come with me to celebrate in my joy and delight! Amen.

Make a list or draw a sketch of some of the things that bring you delight. What do these things have in common? How do you see Jesus in them?

Sadness

Lonely | Guilty | Exhausted
Disconnected | Failure | Grief

Lonely

When you feel lonely, you may feel tired or bored. You feel like you just want to sit down and figure out what to do. But really, you just want someone to talk to. Only at the moment you feel completely alone. Maybe you feel like even God is not there with you.

John 15:13 (NIV)

"Greater love has no one than this: to lay down one's life for one's friends."

My Savior, My Friend by Eliana Wiechman

Growing up, I had three older siblings, so I always had something to do, or someone to hang out with. But as I got older, and they grew up or moved out, we hung out less and less. We stopped liking the same things, and I started having to find stuff to do on my own, by myself.

I would wander the house bored and lonely, wishing my friends could come over, or my siblings would come out and play. Sometimes, I just wanted to talk to someone. Sometimes, I needed help: I was going through something hard and felt alone in it. Sometimes I needed someone to comfort me.

In John 15:13 Jesus calls us friends. And Jesus, our Savior, would lay down His life for us, His friends. Don't be afraid to call Jesus your friend. You can talk with Him, you can share everything with Him. Jesus is your friend. He is your Savior. He is your Shepherd. He loves you and will do anything for you. Most importantly, Jesus will never leave your side. Jesus is always there with you, even if it feels like He's not.

Not only can you talk with Jesus, but Jesus wants to talk with you. God knows that you are imperfect. God knows that you can't carry all of your weight on your own. Because God knows you and loves you, God wants to do everything to help you. Jesus doesn't want you to carry your burdens on your own.

Because Jesus is your friend, you can invite Him to be with you in this time of loneliness. Knowing Jesus is with you may not be everything you need. Knowing Jesus is with you may not cure your loneliness completely. But you may feel better knowing that you have invited your Savior into your loneliness.

Allow yourself to feel lonely, because feeling lonely is okay. Sit with Jesus in your loneliness and ask Him what He is working in your life.

People Like Me

In Daniel 6, Daniel was thrown into a lion's den for praying. (Feel free to read the full chapter on your own.) Daniel was all alone with the lions, but he trusted that God was with him, so he was not afraid. Daniel was in this hardship alone, with no one else around. But he brought his fear and loneliness to God because he knew that truly, God was with him through everything.

You may be like Daniel, alone in a hardship, but never doubt that you can give God your hardships, your loneliness. When you feel lonely, you are not alone.

Let's Pray!

Dear God,

I want to invite You to be with me, to show Yourself in my life so that I can feel You here, with me.

Father, I am lonely. I need someone to comfort me, to help me. Lord, I ask that You would send me someone, whether it is someone I know, or someone new. Shepherd, I need Your help. I cannot go on alone. Amen.

What does loneliness feel like to you? Write down what you feel in your body as well as your heart. Then invite Jesus into each of those experiences.

Guilty

Physical symptoms you may experience with guilt are pains in your stomach, a stabbing in your heart, or heavy arms and legs. You may want to curl up in a ball and cry, or you may want to stand up and yell at anything. Emotions that often accompany guilt are grief, failure, and frustration.

Romans 8:1 (ESV)

"There is therefore now no condemnation for those who are in Christ Jesus."

A Cycle of Guilt by Liz Rossow

(A fake name was used for this devotion)

Sometime mid-January in 2018 I received news that would affect me to an amount I could not have predicted. I was sitting on the couch looking at my phone, probably scrolling through Snapchat, when my mom came over to me. She asked, "Do you remember John from your class in Texas?" And I responded with, "Yes; I remember him." She then said, "A friend who knew him just texted me, and he committed suicide."

I think she walked away after that, but if she said something else I did not hear. I was in shock. John was someone I remember very well from Texas. We were always next to each other in school because our last names start with R.

In fact, he was the first boy I had a crush on. Now five years later, I find out that he died; but even more devastating, he killed himself. Once I was able to speak again, I asked my mom if she had any more information. She did not.

I went up into my room and started to cry. I had no reason, and I got no closure. I just kept thinking about my memories of him. John always made me laugh, and we had a friendly competition in everything.

One memory kept popping up: the day I left. I remember trying to say goodbye to all my friends and teachers on my last day. I hugged and cried with my friends but when I went to look for John, I could not find him. I got in my car and looked out the back window as we drove away. As my school and friends became smaller behind me all I could think about was how I did not get to say goodbye to John.

In my room that night and many nights (and days) to come, this sense of guilt hit me. Guilt that I had left. Guilt that I was not there for him. All the "what if" situations started coming and refused to leave. What if I had never left? Would I have been able to do something to help him? What if I had found a way to contact him in these past five years? Would I have been able to help him?

This guilt followed me around and tainted my memory of him. The red-headed boy in my algebra class kind of looked like John. Every time I logged onto a computer, I remembered racing John when we logged in during computer class, and the guilt was fresh. In the halls, and in the lunchroom; everywhere I went some detail reminded me of my friend. Along with those memories came more and more guilt.

As the days went by, I became aware that I had no right to feel guilty. I didn't even know him. I had no idea if he even remembered who I was. What gave me the right to mourn a person I had not spoken to in five years and who may have not even remembered me? So then I felt guilty about feeling guilty.

Guilt is a never-ending cycle. The first guilt was still there, but now I felt a second round of guilt every time the first one hit. Even when I was thinking about what to write for this devotion, I felt guilty. I didn't feel that I had the right to share this story because so many more people felt the impact of John's death more than I did. They could tell his story better. As the cycle continued, I was ashamed of feeling guilt, and then felt guilty about that.

As you experience this cycle of guilt, know that Jesus meets you there with a cycle of forgiveness. Whether your guilt is justified, unrealistic, sinful, not sinful, or any other variety, Jesus meets you where you are with what you need.

If it takes one time or one hundred times, take your guilt to Jesus. He won't get tired of forgiving you and encouraging you and loving you; so take the time you need, and lean on Him.

You can trust Jesus with your guilt. Jesus wants to hear about what you are experiencing. Jesus will walk with and work in you as you wrestle with the feeling of guilt.

People Like Me

In Luke 5 we hear a story about Jesus calling His first disciples. Jesus called out to the fishing boats that held James, John, and Simon Peter. Following a long night of fishing, Jesus told them to cast their nets one more time into the water. After a brief exchange, the fishermen decide to try it. They pulled up so many fish their nets were breaking and they had to signal to bring the second boat back out to carry everything.

Now who can command creation like that? For these professional fishermen, it must have been obvious that Jesus was somehow connected directly to God. With this realization, Simon Peter tells Jesus: "Go away from me, Lord; I am a sinful man!"

Simon felt guilty to the point of pushing Jesus away. He saw that this man was from God, and knowing his own sin and guilt, he did not want to be by Jesus. But even when Peter wanted to push Jesus away and hide his guilt, Jesus didn't give up on him. "Don't be afraid," Jesus told Peter. "From now on you will fish for people."

That's how Peter first came to follow Jesus: by trying to push Him away. (I love that story!)

We all feel guilty at some point. And, as backwards as it sounds, it's natural to want to avoid Jesus when you feel guilty. But Jesus doesn't give up on people. Your guilty feelings can't keep Jesus from inviting you to follow Him. When you feel guilty, you are not alone.

Prayer

Lord, please enter into my guilt.

Show me how You meet me in my guilt. When I push You away, show me Your loving, never-ending forgiveness.

Please meet my cycle of guilt with Your cycle of grace. Amen.

Exhausted

Exhaustion comes in different ways, and the reasons why you may feel exhausted are different for each person. Stress, especially when it is intense and prolonged, typically yields exhaustion. When I feel exhausted, it feels like I have no energy. I am not necessarily tired or sleepy, but I don't have the energy even to go through my daily life. My eyes feel tired and my head feels fuzzy. My arms and legs may be sluggish, and my heart feels like it is working harder. A lot of the time, I am on the verge of tears for a while before one thing sends me over the edge and I break down from prolonged stress and exhaustion.

Isaiah 40:30-31 (NIV)

"Even youths grow tired and weary, and young men stumble and fall; but those who hope in the LORD will renew their strength."

Hell Week by Naomi Rossow

In our lives, we move so quickly from one thing to the next. Over the course of school, you are preparing for the next grade, which will lead you to the next grade, to the next grade, and so on until you finally finish school and are expected to get a job. Calendars fill up with different activities ranging from a nice relaxing day with friends to a hectic day of work. Free time is consumed by homework or research for this class and that paper. Extracurricular activities claim anywhere from two to ten hours of our after-school time. Life is busy. Life is stressful.

I remember a time in high school when I spent *fifteen hours* at my high school in one day. The day went like this: school from 7:30-2:10 and then musical rehearsal from 2:30-10:30. That was the longest rehearsal of my high school acting career. It was during "hell week," which is when we go through the show from start to finish with all the costumes, makeup, and tech. The rehearsals that week are always longer than any others because it runs through the entire show.

Unfortunately, the rehearsals had already been harder and more stressful than previous years. The musical that year was especially difficult, and when we got to tech week the choreography wasn't even all the way done. We were learning choreography up until the night before the performance. It was terrible. It was stressful. It was long. It was not the fun musical experience I had learned to expect. Instead of the joyful feeling of success, the stress I felt was met with more stress. I was exhausted. I just wanted to lie down, close my eyes, and be out of this situation.

Exhaustion may come as a new emotion to you depending on where you are in your life. You may have never felt this intense exhaustion before. Or maybe you have experienced intense physical exhaustion, but the emotional exhaustion you are experiencing right now comes as a new and unwelcome feeling.

Exhaustion can be confusing because it stems from conflicting emotions. Think about it: prolonged stress or engagement in something causes you to be exhausted, and when that happens you may want to run from or leave those things that are making you stressed. But if those things causing you stress are things you enjoy, then you have the third conflicting emotion of joy coming into play. You are being pulled in at least three different directions by this one emotion (which itself is pretty exhausting!).

When you are feeling exhausted, really the only thing you may want to do is lie down. Talking to people, especially taking the time out of your day to pray, may be the last thing you want to do. But, I encourage you to invite Jesus into your state of exhaustion. Let Him into the hectic moments. Through the haze of exhaustion, spare a short thought toward Jesus. He loves to come and experience your emotions *with* you.

The good news is, these conflicting feelings that make you exhausted will not last forever. Like the verse above says, God will renew your strength. When your strength fails, when your arms drop, when your feet stumble, and when your energy ends, God is there to pick you up and help you along the way.

This does not mean you shouldn't feel exhausted. In fact, it means the exact opposite. Life is stressful and hard. There is no way to get around that. So when your human body and your human emotions are stretched to their limit, God is there to shoulder that burden with you. In your stress and in your exhaustion, call on the name of Jesus. Bring Him into your life, whatever your life looks like right now.

Jesus wants to come give you support. He is working in your exhaustion even though it may feel as if nothing could possibly happen because you are just at your limit. It's okay. Take a moment. Be exhausted in Jesus. Breathe in and out. In and out. Gather your strength and continue through this exhaustion with the promise that God is there right alongside you and the relieving reality that this state of exhaustion will not last forever. Whew!

People Like Me

The people in the Bible are human beings, just like us. They had stressful, busy lives, just like we do; every single one of them, even Jesus. So, instead of giving you a specific example, think of a Bible story you are familiar with and answer these questions about the people in that story. What were they doing? What might their daily lives look like? How might exhaustion present itself in their life? And how did they continue to push through even when the only thing they wanted to do was stop? On the next page, write their names and what made them exhausted. When you feel exhausted, you are not alone.

Use this time and this activity as a little break from your stressful world. Sometimes when I am feeling exhausted, if I stop and take a moment, I will crash, so I keep moving on. Or the stress is so high that the only thing you can do to relieve some of it is to continue to work toward being done with whatever is the source of the stress. If you feel like you can't take a moment right now, then come back when you can and do this activity. It may help you in the future.

Prayer

Dear Jesus,

I am just so tired. Putting one foot in front of the other seems like an accomplishment right now. I don't know how to get my energy back. It feels like an endless loop I can't break.

Please help. Come meet me in my exhaustion because I don't have the energy to come to You right now. I need Your strength. I need You.

It feels like I am on the verge of a mental break. I just have to get through this one next thing. The next step. The next thing. The next assignment. The next breath. Help me to get through these nexts.

Oh, my God ... I need You. Amen.

Exhausted people in the Bible:

Disconnected

When you feel disconnected you might feel like there's no place that you can truly be yourself and be accepted by those around you. You might feel a heavy sadness in your heart as you long to belong and wish there was someone to be there with you. When I feel disconnected, I typically find myself crying and isolating myself more than normal.

Ephesians 1:4-6 (NIV)

"For he chose us in him before the creation of the world to be holy and blameless in his sight. In love he predestined us for adoption to sonship through Jesus Christ, in accordance with his pleasure and will—to the praise of his glorious grace, which he has freely given us in the One he loves."

Outcast by Gabriella Wiechman

For over a year I've struggled with feeling outcast. I've felt like I don't have a place where I belong, and standing out doesn't always feel good.

A year ago I walked out of school on my last day of junior year, expecting to return again after summer break. I assumed I would see my friends again in a few short months as we started our last year of high school. Well, I was wrong in my assumptions. God can make a lot of changes in a very short period of time, and that's what God did the summer before my senior year.

After my parents and I discussed many different options, we decided it would be in my best interest to graduate early as a homeschooler with some "non-traditional" credits. This meant I was done with high school and I could move on to do the work I felt God calling me to: foreign missions.

What I didn't expect was to struggle so much in finding a job to support my mission fund, or even finding a mission organization to travel with long-term. After signing up for several trips and the majority being cancelled because of Covid, I began to wonder what I was supposed to be doing.

I hadn't expected to be home this long in between graduating and leaving the country, so I hadn't really invested in creating new relationships; and to be honest, I didn't have many old ones in the first place. This meant I was left with practically no friends and no church to call my home. I didn't have a community.

I've been looking for places where I can connect with my peers, places where I can feel accepted, but it feels like I keep running into dead ends. It feels like all these places I am looking to make connections are places where I don't belong. It's like my faith causes me to feel like an outcast. I feel like I can't fit in with anyone because of the way I live my life for Jesus. I'm always just "that Christian girl."

It hurts because that's what I love about myself. I love how I love God and others, so when that causes me to be left out or judged it makes it harder to keep living like that.

There are so many ways we can feel disconnected or outcast because of the very things that make us who we are. It may be a special gift you have, the way you laugh, the thing you want to do in life, or even what you are passionate about that causes you to feel disconnected from everyone around you.

It's so hard to be disconnected because we were created by God to live in community, so when we cannot connect with the people around us it hurts. It causes us to live in a loneliness that we were not created to live in.

I want you to know that the feeling of isolation and being outcast that you are feeling is not your fault. It can be so easy to feel like no one likes you because of who you are, but like Ephesians 1 says, God chose you! God chose you before those bullies even knew you.

I know how badly it hurts to be alone and disconnected from everyone around you. Trust me, I know it hurts bad. It's hard to not have someone to go to when you are hurting or excited. It hurts to not have someone to cry with when you're sad or to laugh with when you find something funny. It's so hard to not have a friend to dream with about the things God is doing in your life. It hurts; I know.

There have been many nights where I find myself crying and screaming silently in my room. I feel an unexplainable anger boiling inside of me because I'm so tired of not fitting in, of being disconnected from the people I think should be my community. So I just cry. I curl up in a ball on my floor and I ugly cry. I yell at God because I don't understand why God can't just provide a friend for me. Why do I have to be so alone? Why do all my connections seem weak and inauthentic?

God sees your pain. God sees you when you are crying, and your Father hears you when you are screaming. God sees how you are hurting and how you are longing for people to connect with. Your Heavenly Father knows that you are tired of feeling alone and outcast.

Jesus invites you to feel your pain with Him. Invite Christ into the hurt and the ache and the loneliness. Invite Him into your anger when you find yourself crying alone for another night in a row. Your anger and pain can never scare God away.

God chose you before the world was even created. God adopted you into an eternal family where you belong through Jesus Christ. So maybe you feel disconnected from your friends, or maybe you feel disconnected from your own family; that's okay. Jesus invites you to tell Him about it because you are a part of *His* family.

Jesus doesn't need you to change your hurt or your pain; he's okay with it. But Jesus does invite you to share it with Him. When you share that anger with God, your wonderful Father and Friend delights in sharing that burden with you. You were never meant to be alone, and your Heavenly Father delights in providing for you.

So feel the pain and the anger as you feel disconnected and alone; but also know that God chose you for something greater, and the Spirit of Jesus is preparing something amazing for you, even in this season of disconnection.

People Like Me

I can only imagine the loneliness of the prophet Jeremiah. In Jeremiah 16:2 the LORD says to Jeremiah, "You must not marry and have sons or daughters in this place." And in verse 8 God says, "And do not enter a house where there is feasting and sit down to eat and drink."

Jeremiah was young when he was called. His assignment from God was to prophesy destruction on the land of Judah because of the people's disobedience to God. God told Jeremiah that he was not allowed to marry or attend social gatherings in the place of his assignment. That meant this terrifying calling had to be done alone.

I can't even begin to imagine how disconnected Jeremiah felt in this. To be called to do God's work can already be scary, but to be in a place where you were disconnected from everyone must have been horrible.

This is so relatable because so often we feel disconnected from the people around us, and sometimes the call Jesus has placed on our lives causes us to feel alone in our work.

It is so encouraging to see that Jeremiah felt this, too. He felt disconnected from a community in the work he was doing for God. But even though he didn't have any friends or family with him, he had God fighting for him. When you feel disconnected, you are not alone.

Prayer

Feeling disconnected is hard, and God knows that too. God isn't afraid or intimidated by your anger or pain, so use this as an open space to scream or yell or break something (that you're allowed to break). Let your anger out so that it doesn't have to be bundled up inside forever. If you don't feel able to pray these words, substitute your own or change the ones I've written. Whatever you are able to bring to Jesus right now is more than enough.

God, I'm angry. I'm upset because I'm tired of feeling alone. I'm tired of not having a friend I can trust with everything. I'm tired of crying myself to sleep because I don't have a community to share my hopes and dreams.

Jesus, I know You are good and everything You do is good, and even though I don't see that in my life right now, I'm asking that You come be with me in my hurt and frustration. I need someone to be with me right now, and You are the only one that I feel connected to right now.

God, I want friends. I want people who will encourage me to love and follow You. I want to be connected to the people around me. Provide for me someone who I can be my true self around. Come to me in this loneliness, in this disconnection. Please.

Show me that You are working in my life, even when it feels like I'm alone. I want to see what You are doing in my heart and in my life. Open my eyes to see these things.

I love You, God. Amen.

Failure

You may feel failure in the pit of your stomach. Your shoulders may droop. You may feel tired and unmotivated. You may feel like you have lost hope. The feeling of failure is often associated with guilt or disappointment.

Psalm 103:12 (NIV)

"As far as the east is from the west,
so far does he remove our transgressions from us."

Luke 22:61-62 (ESV)

"And the Lord turned and looked at Peter. And Peter remembered the saying of the Lord, how he had said to him, 'Before the rooster crows today, you will deny me three times.' And he went out and wept bitterly."

Gut-twisting Failure by Liz Rossow

I am a sore loser, and when I fail, it leaves a bad taste in my mouth. From kids' TV shows to honors classes to Instagram posts, the message seems to be clear: hard work can get you where you need to go. (*Be the best version of you you can be!*) I was blessed enough to grow up in a really supportive home that showed me that no matter if I won or lost, succeeded, or failed, I was loved. And yet, even though I live in that amazing environment, I still don't *like* failing.

I have been held to relatively high standards by my family and friends and maybe more importantly, myself. I have always been a good student. Good grades. Good friends. Good relationships with teachers. This made dropping out of physics really hard for me. I wanted to do well. I wanted to climb this mountain and see the other side. I wanted one of those work-hard montages from movies where the characters are bad at something and, one dramatic montage later, they are great at it.

Unfortunately, that was not going to happen with physics. So halfway through the first semester of my junior year, I dropped a class for the first time. I knew it was the right thing to do for my GPA, for my workload, and for my stress load, but it still felt like failing.

I told myself that the reason I dropped the class was that I was moving to online school, starting college, and trying to make new friends. I didn't even have a real teacher! All of these things are also true, by the way, but that feeling of failure was still there. It was just numbed by other stress.

Next came German class. German is the language I have always wanted to learn, and now I had the chance! My dad is mostly fluent in it and could help me. Unfortunately, I didn't ask. I struggled in silence telling myself that if I just focused more or tried harder, tomorrow it would get better. Once again, I wanted a success montage. And again, there wasn't one.

I could not drop the class because I needed the language credit, and I would have been too stubborn to quit, anyway. My grade went downhill pretty fast. As the rest of my life got more stressful, German got pushed to the back burner. It was easier to pretend like it was not a problem than to try and address it along with everything else. Fortunately, I did not get an F in the class, but I was pretty close, closer than I had ever been to failing a class. I was super disappointed in myself.

My GPA and my pride both took a hit. For the second time in one year, I had failed in school. I achieved amazing things in other areas of my schooling and my life, but I had still tried to spin too many plates and a couple dropped. I felt like a failure even though the actual impact was relatively small.

What if you failed at something that was important, like a friendship? What if you failed to keep a promise, or failed to see a real problem? What if your failure affects more than just your own grades, but the lives of the people you care most about? What if you fail to live up to a part of your own identity in a way that hurts your closest friend?

I am talking about the kind of failure that twists your insides until you want to vomit and keeps you up at night, the failure that brings about the deep chest sobs of someone who feels like they are losing everything and knows it is their fault. That failure is much harder and deeper than not getting a good grade or dropping a class.

Whatever brings about the feeling of failure in your life, know that Jesus is there for you. Sit with Jesus in your failure and disappointment. Wonder what God is working in your life and in your heart through this experience. Jesus won't leave you on your own to face your failure.

People Like Me

Peter failed miserably. His name, the nickname Jesus gave him, literally means "the rock." Imagine how much failing Jesus would hurt.

Jesus said to him, "I tell you, Peter, the rooster will not crow this day, until you deny three times that you know Me." Peter had just told Jesus that he would follow Jesus to prison and death, and that was Jesus' response?? Could you imagine your closest friend telling you that you would fail them, not once, but three times, right after such a statement of loyalty?

Later that night, after Jesus was arrested, Peter was sitting by a fire. First, a girl confronted him about being Jesus' friend. He denied knowing Jesus. Then a man confronted him. Peter denied knowing Jesus to him, too. One last time someone confronted him, and Peter denied knowing Jesus for the third time. "And immediately, while he was still speaking, the rooster crowed."

While he was still speaking. The very real signal of his deep failure called out while he was still speaking. I am sure Peter felt his heart sink to the pit of his stomach when he heard that crow. Even worse, "the Lord turned and looked at Peter."

The person he failed was looking at him. The man who warned him that this was coming. I can only imagine that feeling of complete dread. Peter then went and "wept bitterly." Body-shaking, endless sobs. Peter knows that feeling of failure so large and deep he wants to vomit. The gut-twisting pain of failure. Peter, the rock, knows the feeling of failure. When you feel failure, you are not alone.

Prayer

Lord, I have failed. And I hate it!

Come into my failure; come and bring Your amazing grace. Lord, please help me at this time and show me Your forgiving hand. Show Yourself in my failure. Jesus, how are You working in me now?

Amen.

Grief

Grief is the suffocating feeling resulting from losing anything you love. The deep grief that comes from the death of a loved one is especially difficult.

For a teenager, the death of a family member or friend may be the first time you experience the overwhelming emotions associated with deep grief. I remember physical symptoms from grief like losing my appetite, feeling fatigue, and always sitting in a hunched position. You might also feel headaches, stomach pain, or dry mouth. Grief is heart-wrenching.

Grief can be experienced in many ways and for many different reasons. It is not always immediately apparent what causes the emotion.

John 11:35 (NIV)

"Jesus wept."

Overwhelming Darkness by Naomi Rossow

The night a close friend of mine died, I turned my phone off and went to sleep. I knew something was wrong; I knew it had to do with him, and I knew I needed sleep to deal with the coming day.

Before I fell asleep, I prayed, "God be with him. Please let him be okay. Just let him be alive." I woke up the next morning with a worried heart. After I got ready for the day, my dad confirmed what I already knew. On November 8, 2016, at the age 15, I lost a close friend.

The rest of the country remembers that day for a different reason: it was the same day President Trump was elected to office. But for me and my friends, it was the first day of mourning in a haze of gray. Of absolute grief. Of tears and prayers. My life was turned upside down overnight.

I remember very little of the few months after his death. What I do remember is darkness. I remember the overwhelming feelings of sadness, worry, anger, and exhaustion.

About six months later, our youth gathered for a week, staying at the church, serving the community, and making connections. I had built my relationship with my friend at that annual event; it didn't feel right without him there. A gray cloud covered the whole week because of his absence. I missed his arms around me in one of his famous bear hugs.

The tradition of the foot washing was performed on the last night we spent at the church. This was my favorite part of the whole week, and that sentiment was shared by most people. Three stations were set up in the youth room with a chair, a basin of water, and a towel. There was a youth leader at each station. The lights were turned down and quiet music was playing.

If you were the person in the chair, three people prayed over you, but many more than that stood around you with their hands on your shoulders and arms as well as the shoulders and arms of other people around you. My friend had been one of the people to pray over me the year before he died. He called me his sister and hoped we could spend more time together outside of youth group.

The year after my friend died, I prayed over his little brother at that same youth event, not in the formal setting of the foot washing, but to the side of the main event in a corner with a couple chairs. It started with the two of us sitting there alone but ended with almost the whole group of people surrounding us, surrounding him as we shared in the grief of the loss of our friend, his brother.

We stood there supporting him in the midst of an unimaginable grief. He was not alone. None of us were. But I can only imagine that the only person he wanted there with him was his brother.

In the midst of the darkness of the loss of a loved one, there are so many people we can lean on, so many hands to hold and arms to run into. But the only hand we want to hold or arms we want to run into are the ones of the person we've lost.

When we are suffering loss in our life, it is natural to question and blame God. I mean, if the Jesus is the Alpha and Omega, if God is all-powerful, then why did our loved one die? I asked this question many times when I was grieving my friend. I asked "Why him? He was only 15. He had his whole life ahead of him. Why him? Why now?"

If this is where you are in your grief, allow yourself to ask these questions. Do not hide them or shove them down. Shout them out. Let yourself question your God. Embrace your questions. If yelling is where you're at right now, then yell. Give yourself permission to feel whatever you are feeling right now. Do not be afraid to cry or show weakness. In fact, the weakness you think you're showing is the strength of a person who is doing the best she can to survive the unimaginable emotions of death. Everyone experiences grief differently in their life, and every person has the right to their own unique grief.

I also remember anger: anger that I was going through this; anger that my friend was gone; anger that his brother, sisters, parents, and other family were experiencing this grief. My anger increased when I heard the phrase "death, where is your sting?" because I was feeling that sting in that moment. I wasn't mad at the people quoting the verse, but at myself for feeling the sting of death. I mean, Jesus died and rose again, defeating death. Yet, my friend had died, and it stung, a lot. It took me years to realize that even though Jesus conquered death, death still sucks. It still stings. We can rest in the assurance death isn't permanent, but death stings. So let it sting. Don't be afraid to be angry at whoever or whatever you are mad at. And don't let people tell you that you shouldn't feel the sting of death. That sting is still very present.

You may even be feeling guilty. Because people experience grief in different ways, you may see the people around you unable to go about their lives in the same way while you seem to be handling it fine, whatever "fine" looks like for you. Let yourself feel that guilt, but also recognize that people grieve in different ways and, although you are not breaking down in tears every few hours, you are not disrespecting the person you've lost. Everyone will find their own way to navigate the plethora of emotions that accompany the deep grief of losing a loved one.

I encourage you to let God into whatever stage of grief you're at. Even if you are doubting the presence or existence of God, tell that to your ceiling fan as you lie in the surrounding darkness. Your Father will hear you even if your faith is lacking. Invite God into your questions. Prayer does not have to be focused around thanksgiving or requests. Cry to Jesus. Fall on Jesus. Yell at Jesus. Go ahead; it's okay.

People Like Me

John 11 tells the story of Lazarus. Feel free to read the whole chapter, or even the chapters before and after, for context.

The story most people think of when they hear the name "Lazarus" is that of his resurrection, the happy ending of Jesus waking him from his sleep. People tend to focus on the miracle, but look closer: Jesus faced the sadness, anger, and blame of the sisters and the skepticism of the Jews. He felt the emotions you are working through right now.

Jesus grieved the death of His friend. Jesus wept at Lazarus' burial site. I imagine the comfort Jesus wanted was from the friend He had lost.

Jesus weeps with you now. Jesus is not a stranger to death. He knows the overwhelming feelings of pain you are experiencing right now. He was 100% human. Jesus does not leave you alone in your grief. He is present in every tear that streams down your face, in every burst of anger, in every scream, in every question.

The emotions you are suffering through right now will get better. You will learn how to breathe again, how to eat, how to laugh, how to live despite the absence of your loved one. You will establish a new daily routine. You will laugh, cry, celebrate, and fear for reasons not related to this grief. You will remember this person on their birthday and anniversary of death. You will be able to smile at memories of them. I know this message may not reach you right now. I know it wouldn't have reached me in those first few months. Just know, you are not alone. That simple fact can be a game-changer for how you approach your grief. Your God, Father, Protector, Friend is grieving with you as one who has personally experienced grief. That's a powerful statement, don't you think?

When you feel grief, you are not alone.

Prayer

My God,

I have lost a dearly loved person in my life. Their absence suffocates me. I don't know how to go on. Each movement is a struggle. I can't think ahead more than a day. Anger and doubt seep through me as I struggle through the question of why. Why did you take this dear one from me? What good can come from this?

Despite my questions, I ask you to be present in my grief and doubt. I ask that through the feeling of utter loneliness you show your presence to me.

Jesus, I know you wept with Mary and Martha as they suffered the loss of their brother. I ask that you send your Holy Spirit into my emotions. Use those around me as vessels of your love. Share this grief with me because I can't do it alone. I need help to shoulder this burden. Hold me up within the crashing waves of emotion after emotion.

Lord, I need you. Amen.

Grieving a Piece of Myself by Naomi Rossow

When we speak of grief, it is typically in the context of a loved one who has died. However, you can feel grief over losing a placement, situation, item, feeling, etc. Grief is experienced when something we treasured is no longer in our life.

In my opinion, losing a feeling or mindset is one of the most confusing experiences because it is a psychological rather than physical loss. It can be hard to pin down why you are feeling sad or how you lost your former attitude. This type of grief has been common for me during the COVID-19 crisis. When Michigan was practically shut down with the Stay at Home order and I was unable to see my friends or even leave my house on a regular basis, I remember losing the joyful demeanor I had loved about myself. I felt grief over this loss.

There are plenty of reasons you may experience grief over the loss of a mindset or emotion. Just like grief over the loss of a loved one, grief over the loss of a feeling consists of a multitude of emotions, not just sadness. Confusion, anger, and doubt are common emotions in this time of grief.

Whatever you are feeling, bring it to the Lord in prayer. Even if you are experiencing doubt. Even if you feel like a different person. Even if you don't know what your next step is or where it will lead you. Welcome Jesus into what you are feeling. Invite Him to experience it with you. He's ready and waiting, just around the corner, to pick you up when you fall, to help you walk, to give you the strength to continue.

Prayer

Dear Jesus,

I don't recognize myself. I have lost something of important value to me. I feel like a different person.

Please come into this confusion, this grief. Be with me in it. Help me to find myself again.

Lord, I need You. Amen.

Love

Hopeful | Empowered | Special
Anticipation | Romantic | Longing

Hopeful

When you are hopeful, you may feel a sense of giddy anticipation. You may want the thing you are hoping for to come quickly. You may want to smile or even jump at the thought of the thing you are hopeful for. You can feel hopefulness in your chest and bones.

Romans 15:13 (ESV)

"May the God of hope fill you with all joy and peace in believing, so that by the power of the Holy Spirit you may abound in hope."

A Salvation Word by Liz Rossow

I love the feeling of hope. It is an excited anticipation feeling; the knowledge that something better is coming. Hope is a salvation word.

Hope is the focus of many movies, TV shows, and books. Either the characters have to keep hope or they have to find their "last hope." In *The Hunger Games*, President Snow says, "The only thing stronger than fear is hope." Hope is the thing that Snow is most wary of because it is the only thing that can defeat him. Hope is The Resistance's salvation, their most powerful weapon. Similarly, in *Star Wars*, Princess Lea says "Help me, Obi-Wan Kenobi. You're my only hope." She is placing the hope, the salvation, of all the resistance in his hands.

Hoping for summer to come faster does not feel quite as dramatic as being the last hope for a group of heroes in a story. But summer is more likely something you are hoping for. Even in this case, hope is still a salvation word. The thing you are "being saved from" may be *school*, but hoping for summer is still hoping for release from something. Maybe you are hoping to move to a new house or to win a championship. In every situation you are hoping for something, you are also wishing to change a situation you are currently in. This is not a bad thing (most of the time; go to school, kids). Salvation is a key part of our lives and culture.

Since hope is a salvation word, it is fitting that the greatest hope is in Jesus. We have the hope of the Lord, the hope that passes all understanding. We have hope in the Second Coming, the joyful anticipation of the day when Jesus will come again and all believers will live with Christ in the New Creation for eternity. That promise is our hope. In Jesus, we have eternal hope and eternal salvation.

In light of that eternal hope, invite Jesus into your everyday hopefulness. Jesus wants to hear about your hopefulness and encourage your hope. He is your ultimate hope and wants to share in all of your hope. You can celebrate that wonderful feeling of hope with Jesus in a taste of the joy you will feel celebrating with Him after the Second Coming.

Jesus loves it when you trust Him with your hopes and expectations and dreams for something new or better. Jesus is present in your hope.

People Like Me

In Genesis 12, God told Abraham (then known as *Abram*) to leave his home and go wherever God commands. So Abram picked up his life and followed God to Canaan.

When Abram gets there, God tells him: "To your offspring, I will give this land." Then Abram builds an altar to the LORD. He builds this altar to worship, but it is also a sign of hope, hope in the promise that the LORD gave him.

Abram is hoping that one day his descendants will not be strangers in this land. Abram is hoping that he will have descendants to claim the land. This hope is salvation from being an outsider and from having no children. Abram put his hope and trust in God, and God granted him salvation.

When you feel hopeful, you are not alone.

Prayer

Dear Lord,

In this time of hope, be with me. Teach me patience and trust.
Thank You for the hope of ultimate salvation that I have in Jesus.
Come into my hope, I pray. Amen.

Special

When you feel special, you feel loved. You feel like you belong and the people around you really care. Your heart feels warm, and you want to laugh or smile. When I feel special, my cheeks flush and there is a bounce in my step.

1 John 3:1 (TPT)

"Look with wonder at the depth of the Father's marvelous love that he has lavished on us! He has called us and made us his very own beloved children."

God Chose You by Eliana Wiechman

You are special! You are loved! You belong!

1 John 3 says that God lavishes us with fatherly love. You are God's own beloved child! You belong with your God. The Father is your home. You can have peace knowing that you can dwell in God. You are special to God. Your Heavenly Father thought you into being way before you were born. God thought up each and every thing that you are today. If you were lost, God would leave everything to go find you, and to return you to safety. God knows each and every star by name! God knows you by name! Feeling special is a gift.

Maybe it was just your birthday and someone got you a gift. Or maybe it was just a small act that made you feel loved. Many things can make us feel special. It gives you a warm feeling inside, in your heart.

You don't have to feel guilty for liking to get gifts. Accept the gift and just feel good about it. Thank them for it. Thank God for it. Thank your Father for putting that person in your life. Give thanks for everything you have been given that just makes you feel that warmth in your heart, that feeling of being special. Knowing that you are loved and that you belong is such a good feeling!

One Easter my family and I were with our extended family and we were going around the group saying something nice about each person. It didn't have to be anything big, just even a simple "I think you are a caring person," would work. Just hearing those kind words made me feel so special, so loved. It made me smile, and I even felt a little shy with all of the attention on me.

It's just small things like that that can make someone's day: a kind word, a helping hand, a gift. You may not know what is going on in someone's life. Maybe that small gesture could help someone way more than you could have imagined. Or maybe it is even the other way around. Maybe this same thing has happened to you. Someone you didn't even know helped you in a big way.

Whatever the reason you are feeling special today, invite Jesus into that emotion and try and see what He may be doing in your life. God is good. God loves you. Celebrate with your Heavenly Father!

People Like Me

In John 4, Jesus meets a Samaritan woman. Most Jews would never talk with a Samaritan, but Jesus wasn't just any Jew. This Samaritan woman came to the well alone every day. Even the other Samaritan women weren't fond of her, but Jesus took His time to talk with her. Jesus told her that He was the One, the One that they had been waiting for. Jesus chose her out of everyone to be one of the first to know of Him. Jesus, a stranger to this woman, chose her. I imagine the attention from Jesus made this woman feel special.

When you are feeling special, you are not alone.

Let's Pray!

Dear God,

Thank You so much, Lord, for choosing me. Thank You for lavishing me with Your love, for thinking me into existence way before I was born. Thank You for everyone and everything You have given me. Thank You for making me special. I ask that You would help me make others feel special, too. Whether I know them or not, You do. Amen

Empowered

When you feel empowered you might feel like you're being lifted up and encouraged. It feels almost like a bright light in your chest spreading out through your whole body, warming your whole body, giving strength to your body and mind. Your posture might improve and your steps strengthen as a sign of confidence and power. Empowerment and confidence go hand in hand, so it is likely that you will feel one with the other. When I feel empowered, I can feel my chest and chin lift as I walk taller and with more confidence. Empowerment is also relational: encouragement and love from other people increase your confidence. And you can feel empowered to encourage and empower others.

Philippians 4:13 (ESV)

"I can do all things through him who strengthens me."

The Power of a Hug by Liz Rossow

Can't you just feel that long-awaited hug? The one that you have been waiting for because you know that it comes after a long separation or a huge trial? Maybe it comes from a best friend, sibling, or parent but the result is the same: peace. The peace that comes because you know that you are in the arms of someone who loves you, who cares about you, and who will encourage you to keep going. They are empowering you.

I have had many long-awaited hugs. Those most notable are when I see friends that I have not seen in a long time (my best friends from Texas, for example). We see each other about once a year and every time the hugs are so empowering. I feel like I can do anything because I am back with the people I love and who love me. Then there are best friends that I just recently moved away from. They were the people who I spent every day with and then, nothing. Hugs from them are always the best.

Maybe your empowering hug comes after a struggle that was mentally, physically, or spiritual taxing. It could come after a difficult test, a breakup, or an especially hard practice. The newly conquered struggle weighs you down with exhaustion and these hugs overwhelm you so much that even tears may come. When you are held in the arms of your loved one, you feel them lift your spirits and encourage you to continue. You are given the power to keep going forward. They are the empowering arms that form a shoulder for you to cry on or just an embrace to shield you from your troubles.

I remember having a really hard day at school and then having to go to play rehearsal. (This was during tech week, aka "hell week.") I walked down to the theater not jumping and excited as I normally would, but with heavy footsteps. I just wanted to sleep or cry, or both. When I got to the theater, I set down my backpack with a thud and laid down.

Then one of my friends came by and looked at me. She could tell something was wrong because I was very uncharacteristically curled up in a ball on the floor. She sat down next to me and got me to sit up and hug her. We just sat there for a little bit. She embraced me and held me so I would know that I was not alone, and it would be okay. She gave me a place to rest and reset before going onto the next hard task. She empowered me.

God is always there ready to embrace you. Our heavenly Father provides us a place to rest, reset, and be empowered. Psalm 62:5 says, "For God alone, O my soul, wait in silence, for my hope is from him." Even when our world fails us, God's loving embrace never will.

Invite Jesus into your empowerment. He loves you and wants to empower you when you need it most, or when you just need a boost. When you feel empowered by others, rejoice and thank God for those relationships. When you need someone to empower you, turn to Jesus. Ask Him to empower you.

People Like Me

The parable of the Prodigal Son includes a long-awaited hug. The second son squanders all of his inheritance and then decides to come home.

As the Bible says in Luke chapter 15, *"His father saw him and felt compassion, and ran and embraced him and kissed him."* The father ran into the arms of his son and I can only imagine the peace that the son felt in his father's arms. That feeling of release and empowerment is unlike anything else.

In the parable, the son felt so much shame and guilt. He went home not to be embraced but to repent and to maybe become a servant. Even after the long-awaited hug, the son still did not feel worthy; he still tried to tell his father that he was not worthy to be called *son*. The father would hear nothing of it. He commanded that the fattened calf be killed and that a party be thrown, "for my son was dead and is alive again; he was lost and is found." The father looked on his son with compassion and mercy. The father empowered his son when his son had nothing.

When you feel empowered, you are not alone.

Prayer

Dear Heavenly Father,

Thank You for Your empowering embrace. Thank You for always wanting to hold me in my doubt, anger, grief, fear, and joy. Thank You for the people You place in my life that lift me up.

Help me to run home into Your embrace when I need comfort and peace. Thank You for giving Your Son so that I am able to run to You as a daughter, knowing You will comfort me every time.

Send Your Holy Spirit into my heart. Show me what You are working in my life. Help me to lift others up. In Your name, I pray. Amen.

* * *

Empowerment is relational. Make a list of people who encourage you. Then make a list of people you might encourage. Look for ways Jesus is inviting you to interact with people from both of those lists this week.

People who encourage me   People I can encourage

Anticipation

When you are anticipating something, you might notice yourself hoping and dreaming of what could happen. You are focused on the future and how to make it happen. When I am feeling anticipation, my mind is fully activated and my heart rate is increased in excitement.

Joshua 6:16, 20 (NIV)

"The seventh time around, when the priests sounded the trumpet blast, Joshua commanded the army, 'Shout! For the LORD has given you the city!

"When the trumpets sounded, the army shouted, and at the sound of the trumpet, when the men gave a loud shout, the wall collapsed."

Celebrate While You Wait by Gabriella Wiechman

I absolutely love celebrating. If there's a birthday, a graduation, or a wedding, I'll bake a cake and decorate the house because I love celebrating. There's just something about an atmosphere of celebration that makes my heart so happy.

It's really easy to celebrate when there's an event happening. Whether it's celebrating someone's achievements, a winning team, or someone's birthday, I don't know many people who would turn down a good party. But there's one thing almost every celebration has in common, and that's the fact that we celebrate something that has already happened or is happening at that time.

One of the hardest things I've ever had to learn is to celebrate before a victory. In fact, I'm still learning how to do that.

I think a major part of anticipating something is learning to bask in the victory before it even happens. Jesus doesn't break His promises, so when Jesus promises me something, I can trust that He's going to come through with it. That means I can celebrate even before that promise has been fulfilled. This doesn't make a lot of sense at all (faith often doesn't), but let me explain.

My whole family has had a dream from God for a while now that we would live on a large piece of property and use it as a safe space for people to come and reconnect with God and each other. My parents currently run their ministry out of our house, but the dream is to someday run it on acreage. God gave us a promise years ago to provide the land, but as we waited, the excitement faded, and I eventually forgot about the dream.

A few months ago, God rekindled this dream in our hearts and we began to browse the internet for different properties that could work for the dream God had given us. My parents found one that they felt God was calling them to, so a few weeks later we decided to go visit the land, still with nothing more than a promise to hold onto.

Jesus had spoken to us so clearly about his desire for us on this land, and we truly believed God plans to move us onto it. But there's one slight issue: this property was way out of our price range. I mean, *very* out of our price range. Now I know this sounds absolutely insane—trust me, I thought that every morning when I woke up and as we prepared our current house for our "move"—but listen to what God has called me to in this time of waiting for this provision.

Waiting for God to give me my next step in this process, I realized something. God has been speaking to me about breakthroughs for quite some time now, and this is an obvious time for one, but *I have to wait first*. So what could God possibly be calling me to in this time of waiting for a breakthrough?

Oh, yes … celebration! The thing that makes absolutely no sense until you bring Jesus into it.

What I love about the story of Joshua is it shows me why I don't have to be afraid to look foolish in my faith. I've heard this story probably hundreds of times, but it wasn't until recently that I realized *when* the Israelites shouted: Joshua commanded the men to shout *before* the walls came down. They didn't shout the victory cry *after* the city had been taken, but because of God's promise to them they cried out in victory before the promise had been fulfilled!

This is where I get my assurance that I can be excited in my waiting. I can celebrate and trust in the promise even before I see my victory.

When it comes to the property and the promise God gave my family years ago, and even the promise Jesus reinstated in the spring, if you look at our situation now, it seems as if God broke this promise. That's how I felt when we didn't move onto the property right away. But it's been a few months now and, while there is still hope in the promise of that specific land, I've realized that sometimes Jesus uses situations to build our trust in Him. I think sometimes we get upset that God didn't do exactly what we put all of our faith towards.

But God doesn't let our faith and excitement and celebration go to waste. Our Father uses those situations to evolve the promise into something bigger than we could ever imagine. Maybe in my case that doesn't mean a bigger house or more property; but maybe it means deeper friendships and more God-encounters.

So I still don't know when (or if) God will provide the property, and I still don't know what exactly God is up to right now in my life. But what I do know is that my God wants to get excited with me. My Father has a plan for my life that I trust, so I can invite Jesus into my excitement as I anticipate what He has in store for me, even if it looks different than I thought at the beginning of the promise.

People Like Me

"Elisha said, 'Go around and ask all your neighbors for empty jars. Don't ask for just a few. Then go inside and shut the door behind you and your sons. Pour oil into all the jars, and as each is filled, put it to one side.' She left him and shut the door behind her and her sons. They brought the jars to her and she kept pouring. When all the jars were full, she said to her son, 'Bring me another one.' But he replied, 'There is not a jar left.' Then the oil stopped flowing." (2 Kings 4:3-6, NIV)

I can't imagine the excitement the woman in this story must have felt when Elisha said he would help her. She must have expected God to show up in some way, because God worked through Elisha all the time. I can only imagine the anticipation she was feeling as her sons were out gathering jars. She must've known a miracle was coming, even though it might've been hard to believe that God would fill all of her jars with the oil she needed.

How encouraging is it that this woman trusted that God would provide for her needs? Sometimes you might feel alone in your excitement for God's plan for your life, but the amazing thing is, there are so many other people who share that same anticipation. God is doing amazing things, and they are so worth being excited for.

When you feel anticipation, you are not alone.

Prayer

Take this as an opportunity to experience your excitement in the presence of God. Scream at the top of your lungs! Jump and dance in joy around your room! Remember that God loves to celebrate with you!

Hey God!

I feel like You are going to do something amazing in my life soon, and I'm so excited! I can't wait to see what You have in store for me.

I want to tell You about all of the things that excite me about it, because I know how much You like to hear these things from me.

[Now is a great time to just tell God what you're excited about! It might be a date you have coming up, a mission trip, graduation, whatever! Jesus wants to hear about it from you, so tell Him!]

Thank You for listening and caring about the things I'm excited for. I love You, God! Amen.

Write down three to five things you are anticipating in the next five years. Which of those can you celebrate with Jesus, ahead of time?

Romantic

When you are feeling romantic, you probably are continuously thinking about and maybe even dreaming about a special someone. Watching rom-coms and planning your future wedding can be symptoms of romance. For me, romance comes with an exciting sense of beginning and a little bit of fear. I long for a future with my special someone and am impatient for events to play out.

1 Corinthians 13:13 (NIV)

"And now these three remain: faith, hope and love. But the greatest of these is love."

Religion in Romance by Naomi Rossow

I'm gonna be honest: this devotion was especially hard for me to write. There are so many things that go into romance: the giddy feeling that accompanies a new crush or first date, fear that can hold you back from going after the one you want, the good romance from a healthy relationship, and the bad romance that comes with abuse and terror.

Romance can be between two friends who have known each other for years and just started seeing each other in a new way. It can spark between two people who met for just a second. Romance can keep you up at night or give you wonderful dreams. It can grow like a slow fire gradually creeping into different aspects of your life or show up like a quick spark devouring your daily life.

Romance can be new and fun in the first few months, or it can be sweet and comforting after a couple years. It can be the perfect happily ever after with your high school sweetheart, or it can take many trials and errors and finally work with your new coworker years down the line. Romance is so uniquely personal to each relationship and circumstance that it made this devotion insanely hard to write.

I started and restarted writing each time with a different idea in mind. I mentioned my middle school crush and late-night talks with my best friend. I mentioned my parents' gentle romance in our house. I talked about my first kiss. I struggled with the complicated reality of LGBTQ+ romance and Christianity. I questioned what my goal was in this devotion.

Not to be a broken record here, but writing this devotion was hard. So I finally decided just to be honest; to stop trying to write it a certain way or convey in a few pages all the complex messages romance has to offer.

As you read this, know that my past experience of my own romantic life leads me to write the way I do, *and* romance is different for everyone and every relationship. Whatever your experience with romance looks like, I invite you to bring Jesus into it, to seek what He is doing in your life through this significant person in your life.

Through high school I had two boyfriends. With both of them, I didn't know what I was doing, what was expected of me, or what I should be doing. My romance knowledge had come from fairytales and rom-coms, which sadly are not the norm. My first kiss was in the parking lot of my high school, and it was far from the magical moment I had dreamed of. No sparks flew like in the songs. I didn't understand what people were talking about in the books and movies when they mentioned electricity. I liked the way my boyfriend's hand felt in my hand. I liked cuddling up next to him at the movies and driving around in his car, but there was no fire. It was just nice, special.

I was a giddy teenage girl in love. Some girls don't like to talk about it, or they don't even search for romance in high school. I am a romantic and it showed. I remember many late nights with my best friend lying in her twin bed gossiping until two in the morning about our crushes. I am not exaggerating when I say we talked about the same guys for *four years* and then on and off after that. There are many songs I associate with my middle school crush, most notably *My Dilemma* by Selena Gomez. He was a major part of my life for many years. For me, romance is one of the most important (and interesting) things in my life. Balancing that love life with my faith quickly became an issue when I moved to college and the people around me didn't necessarily share my beliefs.

My faith has always been at the center of who I am and guided my actions. I chose to go to a public college for my first year because I wanted to have the chance to live my faith out in a diverse world that had numerous different beliefs. I definitely got this experience. There were moments where I was completely out of my depth and uncomfortably staying in the conversation. And there were other times I was at the heart of the conversation knowing what I was saying and how to say it. I even prayed over a person I met in the Student Center (and never saw him again).

The ups and downs of being a Christian in a non-Christian world were stressful and educational. But when I fell for a junior I met in Dance, I had to really look at what I believed and what was important for me in a romantic relationship. Together we asked hard questions and faced differences in belief. We tackled the fact that I believe in the Bible with a stronger passion than he does. He questions what the Bible says and means in the reality of today. I looked into the theology of my denomination and questioned my own faith; having these conversations with him had opened my eyes that I might not agree with everything my church had been teaching. Needless to say, religion in romance is hard. It's complicated. It's a wonderful thing that takes a lot of work.

Whether you are just starting to explore romance, or stuck with a difficult relationship decision, invite Jesus into your romance. However it looks in your life, Jesus wants to be a part of it. Jesus delights in you. As a giddy smile spreads across your face as your crush takes your hand in the hallway, as the butterflies swarm in your stomach as you prepare to make a move with your long-time crush, or as you sit down for a complicated talk with your significant other, ask Jesus to be present in that moment. Bring Him into your relationship. Send a quick thought Jesus' way; Jesus will be with you and send his Spirit to guide you.

People Like Me

The romance stories in the Bible focus on marriage and family. There are husbands with many wives and wives with many children. Maybe the most famous marriage and family in the Bible is that of Joseph, Mary, and Jesus.

Mary and Joseph were engaged when an angel of the Lord came to Mary telling her she would become pregnant by the power of the Holy Spirit (which I'm sure came with a lot of conflicting emotions). When Joseph found out that Mary was pregnant, he assumed she had cheated on him. Instead of going out and making a big deal of it, Joseph wanted to leave her quietly because he loved her. An angel came to him in a dream to tell him what had happened. When the time came for the baby to be born, they were in a stable in Bethlehem. They were alone. No midwife to guide. No mother to comfort. Joseph and Mary had the baby together and the love they felt was the love of parents, not just that of faithful followers of God.

Imagine being Mary in this story and experiencing all her emotions. The fear that suffocated her when she found out she was going to have a baby. The overwhelming love and gratefulness she felt when Joseph stood by her. I'm sure she felt giddy when getting ready for her wedding (even though it would have been an arranged marriage). I can imagine her struggle over what she wants in her life with her husband. She was faithful to God, even when God's promise didn't look like she expected.

I think Mary felt romantic. It looked different for her than it does for you. It looks different for you than it does for me. Romance is different in everyone's life, *and* when you feel romantic, you are not alone.

Prayer

Because romance is such a complicated emotion and individual experience, I wrote this prayer a little differently. Fill in the blanks in the prayer and take time to pray on your own about your specific situation. Jesus wants to come into your personal life in personal ways.

Dear Jesus,

Thank You for putting _____ in my life.

When I am with _____, I feel _____.

I am feeling _____ (giddy/nervous/scared?) about what comes next. I ask that You please send Your Holy Spirit into my heart to guide me in this relationship, whatever it may look like. For me it looks like:

Take a moment to tell Jesus what is up in your love life right now.

Thank You, Father. Guide me in Your ways, and come to me in my romance. Come, Holy Spirit. Amen.

Longing

When you are longing for something, it might cause you to focus on that one thing and see how it connects to every part of your life. In this devotion I'm going to be specifically talking about longing for some*one* and how to bring that desire to Jesus.

When you are longing for someone, you can probably find yourself thinking about them or imagining what role they would play in your life. When you think of them, you feel a sadness in the waiting, but also an excitement for what is to come.

Genesis 2:18 (NIV)

"The LORD God said, 'It is not good for the man to be alone. I will make a helper suitable for him.'"

Waiting and Wondering by Gabriella Wiechman

They say every girl dreams of her wedding day for her whole life. I've played dress-up-wedding more times than I can count, so that's definitely true for me. But why do we dream about that special day for so long?

God created marriage to be a special bond, in my opinion, between best friends. Do you ever wish for that one person you can tell literally anything to? Someone you don't have to be careful around, someone who truly sees you for who you are. I wish for that person all the time. And I've been talking to Jesus about it for a while now.

For the longest time I didn't care about boys; I thought they were inappropriate and gross. I'm 18 and I don't think I've had an actual crush on a guy before. Maybe I thought I did, but never one where I truly cared for a boy *in that way*. So, as you might've guessed, I've never dated anyone before. I don't even really talk to guys. For the past 18 years of my life that was okay; it didn't matter that I didn't talk to guys because I didn't care about dating. But one day, that switch flipped, and all of a sudden I felt really *single,* and I wasn't okay with it.

I didn't start throwing myself at every guy I interacted with, but I did start noticing guys that I probably wouldn't have noticed before. I realized that I wanted to date someone. When I realized this, I wasn't really sure what to do. I felt like I should talk to someone about it. I wondered if I was supposed to ask my parents' permission to even want to have a boyfriend. Then I realized I was 18 and talked to guys once a year when I volunteered at camp, so I was pretty far from dating anyone.

I decided to take this newfound desire to God, because that's the best thing I knew to do when I didn't understand what I was feeling. I hadn't ever wanted to date anyone before, so why now? Why would God put this desire on my heart when I didn't interact with *anyone*, much less with *guys*?

So a lot of nights I find myself sad and lonely, sometimes curled up in my bed with sad music playing, and sometimes sprawled out on my floor sobbing because I just want someone to love me in a sweet, romantic way. It hurts. It's hard to be single, and it can get really annoying to hear people tell you to "enjoy this season." Because, like most hard seasons, it isn't very pleasant.

The loneliness I've experienced from being single is different than simply not having a friend or being separated from the people you love. Have you experienced that? It feels like you know there's someone out there that God created exactly for you, to love you, but they're on the other side of the world, with no way to communicate with you. It hurts my heart whenever I think about it, and I'm sorry if that's how you're feeling right now. It sucks.

So, why would God give me this desire and nobody to fill that empty space in my heart?

I honestly still don't know that answer, and I still get really, really sad and lonely some nights when I'm trying to go to sleep. But the thing that has helped make that void in my chest feel a little less empty is to talk to Jesus about my feelings and about the desires of my heart. I've also started praying for my future husband, because if I can't interact with him, I sure want God to!

This devotion was one that was really hard for me to write. It took me a while to figure out what to say and how to say it because while I want it to be helpful for you, it is really hard and vulnerable for me. It's hard to admit that you want to date someone; it feels awkward. It's a subject that you don't really talk to anyone about because it feels weird. I want you to know that you don't have to be embarrassed to want what God has planned for you, even if it seems like that thing is silly.

God is in everything, and Genesis 2 suggests that God wants someone for us to live life with, too. God created us to be with someone else.

I once watched a sermon where the pastor mentioned that Genesis 2:18 is the first time in the Bible God says something isn't good. As God created all of the creatures on the Earth, our God always said, "It is good," until this verse. Our Creator knows that we were made to live in connection with someone else in a different way than just having a friend; that's why God created us to be in partnership with another person.

Your Heavenly Father did not create you to live alone, so you don't have to feel guilty when you feel sad about not having someone close to you. Take that guilt and your sadness to your Comforter, because God loves to comfort you and love you when you don't feel that love from someone else. Jesus invites you to tell Him all of the details about why you're upset or sad or annoyed, because He wants someone for you too!

Jesus wants you to have community, so tell Him what kind of person you want to be around. Give Him all of the attributes and characteristics that you are desiring in the people around you and let Jesus hold them safe for you. I've found that giving my desires to God is way more freeing than it sounds.

When you are longing for someone or something, tell God every detail. Plan with your Heavenly Father because your Friend loves to hear your dreams. When you give those dreams that are close to your heart to Jesus, He holds them near to his heart, and Jesus has the power and authority to make those things happen. Even more, Jesus wants to send His Spirit into your heart *and* the heart of your special someone.

People Like Me

I've found that, in the time of waiting and longing for a person to share my life with, I've also grown to long for my Heavenly Father to be near. In a time when it feels so lonely and hopeless it can be comforting to know that there is One who will always long for you.

In John 14:2-3 Jesus says, "My Father's house has many rooms; if that were not so, would I have told you that I am going there to prepare a place for you? And if I go and prepare a place for you, I will come back and take you to be with me *that you also may be where I am*." How reassuring is it to hear that, in your season of longing, there is someone who desires to be with you? It encourages me to know that, even as I feel this longing in my chest for someone to be with, my God longs even more to be with me. So in my loneliness and hope for the future I can know that Jesus is longing to be with me right where I am, and He is preparing somewhere for us to be together for eternity.

As you long for God to send someone into your life, I encourage you to also long for your Heavenly Father, as your Heavenly Father longs for you. Psalm 42:1-2 (TPT) says this:

> *"I long to drink of you, O God, drinking deeply from*
> *the streams of pleasure flowing from your presence.*
> *My longings overwhelm me for more of you! My soul*
> *thirsts, pants, and longs for the living God. I want to*
> *come and see the face of God."*

A friend of mine once said that we have a hole in our heart that we try and fill with other things, but only God can satisfy. I've found that over the past year or so of longing for a partner in life, I have learned to be content with Jesus because I know that out of that contentment I can receive all of the blessings God has for me. Even though I still long for someone to be with, I can know that God has all of that under control. My Heavenly Father will provide just what I need at just the time I need it.

So yes, sit in your longing and tell God all about the desires you have and the loneliness you are experiencing, because your Father loves to hear the things you long for. And I invite you to also look for God's heart in this season. Look for the ways Jesus is filling that hole in your chest with the blessings of the Kingdom, and from that satisfaction learn to ask Jesus what He desires to give you. Because gifts from God are so much more beautiful and amazing than anything we could ever gain on our own. Jesus longs to be with you; so when you feel longing, you are not alone.

Prayer

Below is one of the prayers I wrote in my journal one night when I was really struggling with being single. I want to share it with you because I want you to know that it's okay to want a significant other. And it's okay to talk to God about it! I think it makes Jesus really happy when we include Him in our girl talk.

This prayer is a little bit different and a lot longer than any of my other prayers. When I wrote it one night lying in bed I asked God what to pray for my future husband, and these are the things God told me.

So, as always, I invite you to pray only what you can right now, and to change whatever you need to. Ask Jesus what desires the Father has for you to pray in this season of longing!

Hey God :) Thanks for having someone out there for me. A lot of times I can feel lonely and to know that You have at least one person somewhere that someday will love all of me for who I am without making any changes, someone who wants to commit to spending their entire life with me—that feels really good! I find myself longing for this guy to come around sooner than I guess is Your plan, but I'm slowly learning to be patient because maybe there's some cool stuff You want to do for us that can't happen where I'm at right now, or where he's at right now.

God, I want to pray for my future husband. I pray that You are using this hard and uncertain time to build his character as You are continuing to build mine. I pray that during this time You are molding us to fit even more perfectly with each other. I pray that You would strengthen him to be able to protect me and comfort me, but also to be able to be vulnerable and honest with me, because those things take a lot of courage, too.

Grow him closer to his family right now and surround him with people who are building him up as a man and as a man of God. God, please teach him how to love people like You're showing me right now. Please love him the way You teach us to love others. Help him to not feel alone, but to know that You are always there right with him. Show him the people in his life that he can trust; the people that You've placed there for him specifically in this time.

God, I ask that You continue to grow my future husband up to be the man that You've had in mind since before creation. God, help him to never feel as lonely as I have the past year, but help him also to long for me like I long for him. Help him to respect himself: his body, mind, spirit, and heart. Help him make decisions using the heart that You've equipped him with. Help grow his heart to be strong against adversities and temptations. God, please help him treat himself with love and honor and respect; help him to love who he is because he has been made in the image of Your Son.

Please show up in some crazy, amazing, obvious, breakthrough ways in my future husband's life. Show him who You are: undoubtedly powerful and caring. Help him to be himself fearlessly, no matter what other people say.

And God, it feels weird to ask, but help him to think about me and pray for me. Just like You've put him on my heart, put me on his heart. Maybe he's feeling lonely but give him me to look forward to. God, I'm so excited to meet him! Please put that same eagerness and hope and longing in his heart.

I love You, God; and I'm so excited to love him, too! Help both of us to be smart and aware in our relationships so that we respect each other in everything we do, even though we've never met before. Help him to sleep peacefully and wake up refreshed to do the work that You've called him to do. Amen.

Prayer Experiment

On a separate sheet of paper, write a prayer for your future spouse. Don't worry about how short or long it is, or how deep and intimate it is. Just invite the Spirit to show you the things your Heavenly Father has planned for you. Ask Jesus what He longs for for you in that relationship you are desiring. And then write that down. Save your piece of paper in this book or another safe place to remind you that God is holding your prayer while you are waiting for your future to unfold.

Fear

Inadequate | Uncertain | Nervous
Doubtful | Trapped | Unwelcome

Inadequate

To feel inadequate is to feel like you are not good enough. It can feel like shame or loneliness. I feel it in my stomach, and I feel it in my cheeks; they get red and feel hot. I want to find the nearest corner and scrunch up in a ball. Feeling inadequate can make me very frustrated at myself or angry with other people. Sometimes it makes me cry.

2 Corinthians 3:5 (NIV)

"Not that we are sufficient in ourselves to claim anything as coming from us, but our sufficiency is from God."

Just Not Good Enough by Kate Rossow

Have you ever felt like you were worth nothing or that you weren't good enough for something or someone? My family makes me feel very accepted and loved, but there is always that voice in my head that says, "You're not good enough."

I have two older sisters who are both amazing at everything they do. I look up to them. They were both on the swim team and did theatre at their old school. They get good grades, have amazing friends, and are very confident in themselves. I feel like I am always having to follow in their huge footsteps. I think I have to be like them and act like them because then people will like me. Sometimes I feel inadequate or like I'm not good enough because I come after these legends, and it seems like there's no way I can live up to my sisters.

Sometimes I can feel like I'm not even good enough for God. I feel like I keep failing at what I think is right. I keep trying to change my life, but in the end I still end up feeling like I've let everyone down. I'm a perfectionist, so I always want to have perfect grades, perfect clothes and makeup, and a perfect attitude.

Maybe you feel the same way. Maybe you feel as though you have let down every single person in your life and there is no way you could redeem yourself. In these dark times, Jesus comes to me and to you and invites us to lean on our Heavenly Father.

In 2 Corinthians 3:5, I hear God saying, "Don't be sufficient in yourself because of what you do or how perfect you are, but be sufficient through Me, your Father who loves you. I know you're not perfect. I know you feel as though you couldn't possibly be your sisters. And that's okay. You will mess up time and time again. But I paid for that sin before you were even born; heck, before your great-great-great-great-great-great-great-grandma was even born. I love you and accept you for all of your imperfect features, and it's okay to feel as though you're not enough sometimes, because I am still with you."

The book of Romans says that while we were still sinners, Christ died for us. You can lean on God and know you don't have to be perfect. I know my sisters love me and they don't want me to be them; they want me to be *me*. I believe that it doesn't matter if I have as many friends as they do or if I'm on the swim team. And even though I know these things, it's okay to feel inadequate sometimes. I can bring that emotion to my Heavenly Father who never leaves my side.

People Like Me

At first, when God appears to Moses through the burning bush in Genesis 4, Moses is extremely shocked. But then Moses begins to feel inadequate. He gives excuses like *I can't speak very well*, or *they might not believe me*, and *please, send anyone else!*

Moses! One of the most-known heroes of the Bible!

Moses didn't feel like he was good enough to do what God wanted. But God still promised to be with him.

Even great heroes of the Bible can feel inadequate to do God's work sometimes. That shows me it's okay for me to feel inadequate, too, at times. I'm just glad God promises to go with me, even when I don't feel up to the task or when I don't feel like I can face people who might not like me. And especially when I feel small and scared on the inside.

When you feel inadequate, you are not alone.

Prayer

Dear Jesus,

Please help me to lean on You and know that You love me no matter how imperfect I am. Please help me not to feel pressure to be someone I'm not; and please be close to me when I feel like I have disappointed everyone.

Lord, show me that You are near and that I don't have to be perfect. Remind me that it's okay to feel inadequate, and thank You for helping me feel sufficient through You. Your will be done. Amen.

Prayer Experiment

I hate feeling inadequate! So I hate talking about what makes me feel inadequate! Even with Jesus!

But it's also really helpful to get those feelings off your chest. Take a minute to list some situations that make you feel like you aren't good enough (but write them backwards, so other people can't read them at a glance!). Then ask Jesus what He thinks about you in each of those situations. What matters most to Him? Invite Jesus into the places you feel most inadequate.

Uncertain

When you are uncertain, you may have anxiety or feel nervous. Lack of confidence is another sign of uncertainty. Your heart beat may increase. Dry washing your hands or unsettled hands could be an indicator. You may feel this emotion as an uncomfortableness in your stomach or heart area.

Isaiah 41:10 (ESV)

"Fear not, for I am with you;
be not dismayed, for I am your God;
I will strengthen you, I will help you,
I will uphold you with my righteous right hand."

Cradled by God by Liz Rossow

In early May of 2019, I was sitting in my room surrounded by piles of boxes full of my stuff and watching songs for our summer VBS. Because I was a part of the team that leads the actions, I had to learn them beforehand. One of the songs I was watching repeated these lyrics:

> *There is a whole lot of change coming your way,*
> *'cause like it or not nothing stays the same.*
> *So hold on tight and follow real close,*
> *'cause God is good and He's in control.*

I started laughing with a heavy heart as I looked up toward the sky and said, "Okay, God; I get it. Everything is about to change. Thanks for the heads up."

Half a year earlier, my dad told my family he was planning to resign his position as a parish pastor to write books and create other resources that help people take a next step following Jesus. Over time, God seemed to have been calling him in that direction, and Dad wanted our input. As much as it meant our lives would get up-rooted, we agreed that this was our next right step.

In the months to follow, we would sell our house, leave our church home, and move in with my grandma. I would start online school for my junior year of high school, start an online college program, find a new theatre program, leave old friends, meet new friends, and have my older sister move away to college. The VBS song was playing on repeat:

> There is a whole lot of change coming your way,
> 'cause like it or not nothing stays the same.
> So hold on tight and follow real close,
> 'cause God is good and He's in control.

This is not the first time my life was uprooted and moved around. I moved from St. Louis to Texas when I was four, and from Texas to Michigan when I was nine.

Yet, this time was different. We didn't know where we were going when we set out. It's been a year, and we still don't know where we are going. We are still stuck in limbo between where we were and where we will be. All of the other moves had a new school and church waiting for us because that was why we were moving. This time, we were moving into uncertainty instead of just a different situation.

Through this long time of change, a new kind of uncertainty became a part of my everyday life. Rather than simply having the uncertainty of moving, we were facing the uncertainty of moving plus the uncertainty of moving to a rest point rather than the final destination.

As a pastor's kid, I am used to an underlying knowledge that I may not be where I am at the end of the year, the uncertainty that meant all my plans may be for nothing because I could live half way across the country in a few months. But I still planned. That uncertainty was something you don't address until it's happening. The new uncertainty was smacking me in the face every day. Almost every question people asked me about the future, even just the next few months, was answered by, "I don't know." It was terrifying.

I remember crying myself to sleep many nights because I just knew nothing. Those nights were the nights that I would pray out loud until I fell asleep. I am not sure if the prayers were coherent or not. They were definitely repetitive. I would pray, "Lord, show me where You want me to go. Show me what comes next. I am terrified. Lord, help me. I know this is what You want my family to do, but why? Why? Why?"

One of those nights, I felt this heavy weight on me. It was not like a boulder crushing me. Instead, it was like a big comforter being laid on me during a cold night. I felt the hand of God holding me as I cried. I was rocked to sleep in the arms of God as a child is rocked to sleep in the arms of a loving parent. Every night after, when I would start to panic or cry in my bed, I would feel the heavy Presence and I would be wrapped up and held until I fell asleep.

No matter what you are feeling uncertain about—whether it be a move, family turmoil, a divorce, a death, or maybe something in your control like an especially hard decision, an important class, or a new job—your heavenly Father is there to hold you and guard you as you go forward. When you feel uncertain, bring God into it. Feel free to say whatever is on your mind: suffocating fear, angry questions, sorrowful confusion, anything at all! Bring Jesus into your uncertainty and be wrapped in the Father's loving arms. As the song says …

> *So hold on tight and follow real close,*
> *'cause God is good and He's in control.*

People Like Me

Gideon was chosen by God to help free God's people from the Midianites. His story is told in Judges 6-8. After being chosen by God, Gideon was facing uncertainty, and he felt it. He did not know what the LORD was going to ask him to do, and he did not know the consequences that could come from the Midianites.

Gideon was so uncertain of the path the LORD had set before him that he tested the LORD. Gideon asked that the fleece he laid out be wet with dew but with none on the ground around it. God was faithful and made the dew appear only on the fleece.

Gideon was still uncertain. He asked God to do the reverse: to have dew land only on the ground and leave the fleece dry. Once again God was faithful; the next morning the dry fleece was surrounded by wet ground.

Throughout Gideon's time serving the LORD, he was uncertain. He questioned the LORD's plans. Through Gideon's doubt and uncertainty, the LORD was faithful. God used scared, doubtful, uncertain Gideon to fulfill God's plan and save God's people from the Midianites.

When you feel uncertain, you are not alone.

Prayer

Dear Heavenly Father,

In my uncertainty, I look to You.

Help me trust You at this time. I do not know what is coming. Help me to trust in You and in Your promise that You have good things planned for me. Help me to follow You and take each step with Your hand guiding me. Comfort and hold me until Your plan is revealed to me.

Send Your Holy Spirit into my heart. Work in me. Use my uncertainty according to Your will. Come, Jesus. Be near me. Amen.

Prayer Experiment

The things I feel uncertain about tend to leak all over the place: I find myself thinking about them or stressing about them all the time, even when I can't do anything about it.

Write down a few things you feel really uncertain about. Then draw a circle around them. By enclosing them with that circle, you are setting a limit on how much time and emotional energy you will spend on them. You can leave them in that circle and come back to them later. Jesus has them safe and sound; He'll be glad to talk about them when you are ready.

Nervous

When you're nervous, it can cause you to overthink a lot of minor things and forget to trust God and God's plan because you are so worried about you and your plan. When I get nervous, I notice shaking, sweating, and an increased heart rate. This devotion focuses on feeling nervous about the future and the plans God has for you.

Genesis 13:16 (NIV)

"I will make your offspring like the dust of the earth, so that if anyone could count the dust, then your offspring could be counted."

Genesis 16:1-2 (NIV)

"Now Sarai, Abram's wife, had borne him no children. But she had an Egyptian slave named Hagar; so she said to Abram, 'The LORD has kept me from having children. Go, sleep with my slave; perhaps I can build a family through her.'"

Spoiled Plans by Gabriella Wiechman

I turned eighteen earlier this year, which for most people would be a really exciting moment, but it was a little different for me. My birthday was the last free day for me before quarantine started. This meant I was going to have a lot of time to think about what I wanted to do with my life.

I've been struggling for over a year now with what God is calling me to do; every time I thought I knew God's plan, things went sideways.

When high school ended for the summer, I was planning to return in the fall for my senior year. It didn't work out that way.

I was excited to be returning to summer camp for my second year as junior staff. I really felt like God had something big planned for me, but camp this year turned into one of the most emotionally challenging two weeks of my life. I went expecting it to be one thing, but it wasn't that at all.

When I got home from camp, I was so confused why God would let something I was so excited for turn into something that hurt me and actually took away my energy. I was tired and sad and upset with God for a while after that, but I know that God is good, so after a week or two I was back to being excited for what God had in store for my future.

At the beginning of July, I was beginning to wonder if public school was really what I was supposed to do for my senior year, but I wasn't ready to make any changes because I wanted that experience. I wanted to go to pep rallies, homecoming, and prom. I wanted to walk the stage for graduation and go celebrate with my friends.

Before I made any decisions about school, I had another trip to prepare for. This time I was going to National Youth Gathering (NYG) in Minneapolis, Minnesota with my youth group. I was a little bit hesitant to be hopeful for a good trip because of what happened with camp, but I still felt like God had something in store for me, so I got packed and my friends and I were excited to go on a trip together and praise God!

Sadly, this was another trip that just didn't hit the mark. There was so much tension and anger in our group. Everyone was tired and upset with each other, which caused a lot of hurtful words. A day or two into the trip I called my mom and just cried. I was in the middle of a room filled with laughter, friends, and games, and I was crying on the phone to my mom. I didn't understand why God would have the two things I was looking forward to go sideways. Especially when I was hoping for God to do something big. Why would my Father shut down my hope? Why would God ruin the only things I had to be excited about?

Once again, I found myself in a place of hopelessness. I was mad at God, I was mad at my friends, and I was mad at myself for being mad at God and my friends. I tried to focus on the positives. And I did make some amazing memories at NYG. I got to catch up with old friends who lived far away. I truly experienced God there in Minneapolis. But none of that seemed to matter, because this felt like just another failed plan.

It's hard to keep trusting God's plan when everything you look forward to falls apart. After a few failed plans, I began to get nervous that I was doing something wrong, like maybe I wasn't doing the thing God wanted me to do and I was messing it up.

When I got home from my trip, I was exhausted again. I was tired from being mad. I was tired from crying. I was tired of crying and being upset with God and the people around me. I just wanted one thing to go the way I thought it would, or maybe even better than I thought it would!

At this point, I was still pretty upset with God, but I wasn't ready to give up hope. I just wanted to see God do something big in my life, and I knew that would happen. I ended up choosing *not* to go back to public school, and, after going through many options, I decided graduating early as a homeschooler with some non-traditional credits was the way to go. I wanted to give God room to work. (Not that God needed it, but I did. I needed to have the space to see every little thing as a God moment.)

I was so excited for what God would provide. I started trying to get a full-time job ... but that didn't work out. I signed up for several mission trips ... but two of the three were cancelled due to COVID. Instead of going on multiple international mission trips, I ended up being home a lot, not making very much money, and wishing I was travelling and meeting new people. It was a very lonely and hard time for me.

I'm not going to lie, I'm still in that season. I don't have very many friends, but the ones I have mostly live far away. I still am home a lot. Every time I seem to hit a groove where I'm making money and feeling included in a community, I seem to run into a wall.

Recently, it's been really hard for me to stay hopeful in God's plan. I still believe that God has something big planned for me, but it's getting harder to trust that my Father will come through. I've started to have almost a surface-level hope for things. I act hopeful and talk like I'm expecting something great, but in my heart I'm really just expecting more disappointment.

I wish that I could continue to trust God and God's plans for me, but when every plan gets cancelled and every event goes wrong, it's hard to keep getting my hopes up. I'm nervous that if I continue expecting big things and being hopeful, then my heart is going to keep getting hurt by broken expectations.

There are so many Bible verses that tell you how God is always in control and God's plans are different and greater than ours, but to be honest, that's not what I need to hear. I know those things. Those facts are stuck in my mind and heart, and I believe them completely. But what I need to hear when I'm nervous about my future and what it does or doesn't hold for me is that I'm not alone. I need to know that it's okay to be nervous, because God can still be near to me even when I'm worried. Maybe you need to hear that, too.

My nervousness or lack of hope does not scare God away. My unwillingness to follow God's plan because I'm scared that it won't go well cannot mess up God's plan. I cannot ruin God's plan. No matter what.

People Like Me

I think Abraham and Sarah must have struggled with this, too. God promised them offspring as many as the sand on the shores of the beach. That's a big promise! I can imagine when God told Abraham that, he was pretty excited. He probably expected God to fulfill this promise immediately. But as time went on and Abraham still had no children, we see the hope and the trust start to fade. When he still had no children, he spoke to God again, asking if the promise would be fulfilled. God explained what the promise was, and Abraham believed.

Years later, when Abraham and Sarah *still* had no offspring, they decided to make a plan of their own. This is exactly what I'm nervous about. I'm nervous that if God continues to change my plans and if my heart keeps getting hurt by feeling like God isn't coming through, then I'm going to resort to making my own plans. I'm nervous that I'm going to give up on God's plan because it isn't happening soon enough or isn't good enough for me. I'm worried that will mess up my Father's promise.

I think Abraham and Sarah must have known their plan wasn't what God intended for them. But I understand why they did it anyway. When your hope is shattered enough times, you start to believe that God isn't going to follow through.

Abraham and Sarah gave up on the promise. They decided God wasn't going to do what the promise said God would do. Here's my favorite part of this story, though. After Abraham and Sarah did their own thing, and realized they had messed up, *God still came through.* It took even longer, but God still fulfilled this divine promise.

Abraham and Sarah messed up. Big-time. But God made a promise. If there's anything I know about my God, I know my God keeps promises. It might take a long time, and you might make some mistakes, but God never takes back a promise.

In Genesis 21:1 it says, "Now the LORD was gracious to Sarah as he had said, and the LORD did for Sarah what he had promised. Sarah became pregnant and bore a son to Abraham in his old age, at the very time God had promised him."

Abraham and Sarah had to wait 25 years from the time of the original promise to the time Isaac was born. They lost hope in the middle. They did their own thing because they didn't trust God to do the thing God promised. But God didn't abandon them when they messed up, and God didn't take back the promise when Abraham and Sarah lost focus. God still showed up.

I know that I'm going to mess up as I'm waiting for my promise to be fulfilled, but I also know that in my worry of messing up God's plan, my Heavenly Father is still there for me. I don't have to be nervous that I will mess up God's plan, because I can't. But I don't have to fix my nervousness in order for God to be with me; God stays with me even when I'm nervous, and God is there for me as I learn to trust God's promises again. When you feel nervous about the future, you are not alone.

Prayer

God loves to hear your voice, even when you are struggling to trust what's next. So whatever words you are able to share with your Heavenly Father right now are more than enough. If you can't pray this prayer, that's okay. If you can only pray one part of this prayer, that's okay. Just know that whatever you bring, God will delight in hearing from you, no matter how much you are able to share.

Father,

I keep finding myself worried that You aren't going to do what You told me You would do.

I'm angry. I'm sad. And I'm tired of feeling that way. I wish I could just trust you to deliver like I've seen you do before, but I just can't right now.

God, please help me to know that it's okay to be upset. Help me to know that you have a plan, and I can't mess it up. Help me to believe in your promises again.

Rekindle the fire I had when you first told me your promises for me. Help me to be excited again for everything you have in store for me.

I love you, God, and I'm ready to be hopeful again. Amen.

Doubtful

The feeling when some aspect of your faith, personality, or life in general is unsure. Confusion and frustration often accompany feeling doubtful. When I experience this emotion, I get tired earlier and sleep longer and more restlessly.

Matthew 28:17 (NIV)

"When they saw him, they worshipped; but some doubted."

Divine Intervention ... or Not by Naomi Rossow

Doubt in faith is a complicated thing. I mean, just the words themselves contradict each other: doubt *in* faith. A doubting heart can manifest itself in many different ways.

You could be doubting your parents and their wisdom, telling yourself that they don't know what it's like to be a teenager these days, and you clearly should be able to make these decisions on your own.

Or you could be doubting your friends and their loyalty to you. I mean hey, if Tiffany was talking to Jessica the other day then she is probably gossiping about someone, and you just told her that really huge secret about yourself. (Don't worry; I won't tell.)

Or you could be doubting your significant other. Chad got three phone calls yesterday while you guys were together and wouldn't answer the phone. Something is clearly wrong.

Maybe the most difficult one to understand, you might be doubting God. The things you want to change in your life stay the same, and the things you want to stay the same change. How does that make sense? Doubt in faith is hard. It's confusing. And it's complicated. What sparked the fire of doubt that is now raging in you? Thankfully, you don't have to deal with it alone.

I am 19 years old. I have lived in 3 states and 7 houses (8 if you count my college dorm). My childhood was spent in St. Louis, Texas, and Michigan. I grew up in a family that moved when God said move and stayed when God said stay no matter what, even if it was the harder path to take (which most of the time it was). I grew up with a strong faith walk and unconditional love being modeled for me by my parents. And yet, I have experienced doubt in faith.

When the coronavirus first shut down my state, I was overwhelmed. The emotions I had were clouded by confusion. I wasn't sure what was happening or what would happen next. I was forced to move back into my parents' house two months before I was planning to. I shared a room with my little brother, and my clothes were in a dresser in the hallway. It was so much all at once. My head and heart were overwhelmed, so I just tried to take it one step, one week at a time.

Soon after that, I began to doubt. I fell into a state of sadness and anger. I didn't want to get out of bed. I didn't want to "go to class" on my computer. I was tired of being in the house, in my brother's room. I wanted to see my boyfriend and my friends again. I didn't understand how my family could just pretend like nothing had happened. But most of all, I couldn't comprehend why God would let this happen.

I would lie in my bed every night and silently (because my brother was asleep in the bunk below me) yell at God. Yelling about the virus sweeping across the world leaving chaos and death in its path. Yelling about the fact that I had to be silent in my pain because my baby brother was asleep. Yelling because I didn't understand what was happening. Yelling because I didn't want to feel this way.

And, in that angry yelling, doubt crept into my heart. I doubted the power of God. I mean, if the King was *all powerful* then why were so many people dying isolated from their family? And then, I started to doubt the faithfulness of God. If God was faithful then why would we be abandoned to the hands of stressful, world-wide decisions and deadly viruses? I even started to doubt the existence of God. How could any of this happen if there was a God?

I honestly can't tell you how I got out of it. There wasn't a divine intervention with flashing lights and booming voices. My eyes didn't miraculously open to the truth. I wasn't slapped into shape by my friends or family. There was no defining moment where I remembered my faith. Instead, it was a slow, almost unnoticeable change in my mindset. I started to feel happy again. I finished my classes (with all A's too!) and was proud of that accomplishment. The sun made a more regular appearance, and I spent more time outside. The restrictions loosened, and I was able to see my boyfriend again. And, with the uplift in my general attitude, my faithful mindset returned. I stopped shouting at the ceiling. My questions about God lessened. I was able to talk confidently about my faith again.

There was no big gesture that drew me back to my faith. There was no miracle. The Holy Spirit worked in my heart, just as in yours. The Spirit works despite our doubt.

As you experience all different kinds of doubt in your life—from the unsettling doubt in a friend to the heart-wrenching doubt in your God—allow yourself to feel it. Don't suppress it. It will come back to bite you in the butt if you do. Give yourself permission to scream and shout. Ask all the questions that flood your head as your heart doubts. Shout at your ceiling. Ask your ceiling fan the hard questions you have never thought of before. Because God will hear your desperate cries, despite your doubt. The Spirit will continue to work in your heart in your doubt.

Doubt. It's hard. It's complicated. It's confusing. And *it's okay*.

This will not be the last time you experience doubt. Unfortunately, doubt is a natural part of life. As you have new experiences and meet new people, you will doubt again. You will ask questions. Your faith will change. That is all okay. It is all welcome. God welcomes your questions with open arms. They are an opening for the Spirit to come work in your life and your heart in a new way. So, tonight as you are doubting, give yourself permission for that to be okay and experience your emotions and questions to their fullest.

People Like Me

The twelve disciples are known for their role in the ministry of Jesus, so it makes sense that they would be strong in their faith walk, right? But there are actually a lot of examples where they were doubting. Even at the very end of the story.

Do you remember the famous, "Therefore go and make disciples of all nations, baptizing them in the name of the Father and of the Son and of the Holy Spirit" from Matthew 28? Just two verses before that, the Bible tells us that some of the disciples doubted. The Great Commission is one of the most well-known verses in the Bible, but we don't talk about the doubting hearts who were there to hear it.

Give yourself permission to feel your doubt. You are not the only one to feel doubt. You are not the last one to feel doubt. You will most likely experience doubt again. When you feel doubt, you are not alone.

Dear ... Someone

Take this mini monologue and read it to yourself or to your ceiling fan. Add anything you want to it. Take anything away. God is listening even if you don't see that right now. It's okay.

Dear ... Someone,

So I am having a really hard time understanding right now. I mean, if God is all-powerful, then why is my life in ruins like this right now? I can't comprehend what is happening. The equation does not add up.

Where I used to talk to an understanding and loving Father, I am now crying to myself in my room, hoping the lamp on my dresser will understand. What is this? Why? I wish this wasn't happening in my life.

Amen...?

Emotion Experiment

Answer these prompts, preferably out loud, to give your thoughts direction and maybe some emotional clarity.

- Who am I doubting?

- Was there a specific event or situation that triggered this doubt? If so, what was it?

- How is my doubt manifesting itself in my daily life? Is it affecting my sleep and/or eating habits?

- Is there someone I can talk to about this? If so, can I call them right now? (If you can, do it! Talking to a trusted person is a great way to sort out what is happening and how you're feeling.)

- What is my next step in this doubt? Writing? Talking? Crying? Analyzing? Yelling? Sitting? Music? Sleeping?

Trapped

The feeling that you are stuck in one moment or place in time. The feeling that you can't escape a physical place or emotional state. When you feel trapped, it can get hard to breathe and you could feel lightheaded. You might feel as though you don't belong anywhere you go.

Ecclesiastes 9:12 (NIV)

"Moreover, no one knows when their hour will come: as fish are caught in a cruel net, or birds are taken in a snare, so people are trapped by evil times that fall unexpectedly upon them."

Emotionally and Physically Trapped by Kate Rossow

Sometimes it can be easy for me to feel trapped. I feel stuck in one place and like there is no way to escape my destiny and my future. I look around at my life and I say, "Kate, where are you? What are you doing with your life? Why aren't you doing *this*? Why aren't you doing *that*?" I feel lost and trapped.

In my eyes, you can either feel emotionally trapped or physically trapped. I have felt both multiple times. One time that I feel physically trapped is when I think about all of the big dreams I have for my life.

Do you have a big dream? Do you ever imagine a life you could have? Maybe you have a particular place you would like to live or a certain job you would like to have. Perhaps you would like to get rich and live in a mansion. Or you could have a dream that you are so embarrassed about you haven't told anyone.

I have a dream kind of like that. I really want to move to New York. I want to see the tall buildings and the virtual ads. I want to see giant faces staring down at me from billboards. I especially want to walk down Broadway looking at the gorgeous theaters and imagining walking out the stage door and having fans cheer as loud as they can.

Imagining this, I get to feeling trapped here in Michigan. Don't get me wrong; I love it here. I just feel like God has such big plans for me and I get anxious to get going on those plans. I feel as though I could be doing so much more if I wasn't trapped in this box. Since I am only thirteen, I basically still have to do what my parents say and go where they go, which can also make me feel trapped as the "daughter of the Rossows". Sometimes I even feel like I belong somewhere else, but can't escape where I am, physically. This is how I would describe feeling trapped.

Dealing with the emotional side is also very trying. When I feel emotionally trapped, I feel as though my brain only knows one command. It's like the same emotion is on repeat: I am in this constant loop of *bleh*.

Sometimes I would even call it feeling *weird*: you're not really sure what the exact emotion is, all you know is that you are trapped in a cycle of uncertainty. In some instances, I have felt like I'm just watching a movie of my life. It's just a constant drag.

One of my favorite things to do in these states, and the most comforting thing, is to pray. I tell Jesus about all of the plans I have for my life and ask Him to give me patience. I tell Jesus about all the amazing places I want to see and visit. I tell Jesus that I want Him to do great things with my life, and I give Him the wheel to do with my life as He sees best.

I always like to go back to Jeremiah 29:11-12. "For I know the plans I have for you," declares the LORD, "plans to prosper you and not to harm you, plans to give you hope and a future. *Then you will call on me and come pray to me, and I will listen to you.*"

Now notice how God does not say, "Everything will go perfectly in your life and you will get everything you want." In fact, Jeremiah is telling us that God will be by our side even when we are feeling trapped. God will listen to you when you pray, no matter what's going on in your life. God can even take things that hold us back and use them for good.

Jesus is also inviting you to find comfort in talking to Him and sharing your dreams. You know how your parents always want to know what's going on in your life; they want to talk to you and listen to you and be a part of your life. Our Heavenly Father wants that, too. Share your thoughts with your Father. Feel your feelings, and know that God knows what you feel, even when you feel trapped.

People Like Me

Okay; so, talking about real life for a second here, COVID sucked. Quarantine was like being trapped in a small space for a really long time, not knowing when you could leave, and not knowing what would happen, all while seeing people die around the world. Hmmm … I wonder what that reminds me of?

When the world had fallen into complete and utter evil, God decided to wipe out the human problem and start over; but not completely. There was one family left on the earth who loved God and decided to continue following their Heavenly Father. The main guy's name was Noah, and God asked him to build a giant boat, or ark. Sound familiar?

I am sure that Noah and his family felt very trapped while waiting in the ark for a sign from God. They were probably in a small space for a really long time, not knowing when they could leave, and not knowing what would happen, all while people died around the world.

But here's the thing; the story doesn't end there. We are told that after those long, long days and nights, there is a light at the end of the path. God made a promise to Noah, saying a flood would never cover the whole earth again. To seal the deal, and add a cherry on top, God created the rainbow so we remember the promise when we see its colors.

God has also made a promise to us: Jesus will come again. There will be trumpets blaring and the mighty King will take us home. He will create a new Heaven and Earth for all who believed in Him. To seal the deal, and add a cherry on top, Jesus pours out the Spirit to give us faith, hope, and trust in our everyday lives. This darkness we experience now will not last forever. There is a light at the end of our path. Come quickly, Lord Jesus; we miss you. When you feel trapped, you are not alone.

Prayer

Dear Jesus,

Thank You for sustaining me through the waiting and wondering. Please help me to turn to You when I feel trapped in my own emotions and bad habits. You are greater than any worldly thing that could happen. I believe there is a light at the end of this path. Be with me throughout this emotion and help me to come to You with all I feel. Pour out Your Spirit on me again today. Your will be done, Lord. Amen.

Unwelcome

When you feel unwelcome, you might feel different or left out. Maybe there's a group you want to be in, but you don't feel accepted. Or maybe in your everyday life you just don't feel like you fit in. When I feel this way, it causes my heart to ache, and I feel a heavy, sad feeling in my chest. I feel like I have to hide myself or pretend to be someone else to fit in.

John 1:10-11 (NIV)

"He was in the world, and though the world was made through him, the world did not recognize him. He came to that which was his own, but his own did not receive him."

Unknown by Gabriella Wiechman

A few months ago my cousin, Jordan, and I were tired of sitting around and doing nothing in quarantine. We wanted to go do something productive, so we went out and got a job working at a PPE factory close to home. It was a full-time assembly line job, eight hours a day with a one-hour lunch break.

Those days were some of the longest days I've ever worked, and we had to wear a mask and hairnet the whole time, which made it even harder. But the thing that made me the most uncomfortable was not the mask, the hairnet, the gloves, or even standing on my feet all day, but it was the fact that Jordan and I were the minority.

We were in a situation where we were easily the youngest people in the room, and we made up a very large portion of the women there. When we walked into the room, we stood out; and that made me nervous.

I had a lot of conversations those weeks at the factory. I talked to so many different people who came from extremely different backgrounds and heard so many inspiring and heart-wrenching stories. I loved getting to share my story with the people I met because I was able to tell them about the work Jesus has done in my life. But most conversations started out something along these lines:

"So, what's your name?"

"I'm Gabby; what's your name?"

"I'm ___. So, you got a lot of money or what?"

Or: "Is this your first job ever?"

Or: "You walk a little different with those expensive clothes on; how much did those cost?"

At first it wasn't too bad, but after most of my conversations started like that, I began to feel more and more out of place. I had never had to defend my work ethic to someone before. Everyone who knows me knows I do a good job and I love to work hard, so when my coworkers started assuming I was rich and lazy from how I looked rather than how I acted, I felt ostracized.

I felt like suddenly I stood out in a not-so-good way. I knew that I was a hard worker. I knew that I'd had plenty of jobs before that. And as far as my clothes went, I knew I didn't buy anything that cost more than $10 if I didn't absolutely have to.

I didn't like that my personality and morals were being stereotyped by my age, race, and gender. Maybe you've been in a situation like that, too. You feel like other people assume they know who you are based upon how you look. Here's a short clip from my journal one of those nights:

> "When my heart and personality come under attack,
> even if the people attacking them don't realize how
> hurtful that is or that they are even hurting me in the
> first place, I don't want to be there anymore."

Feeling unwelcome comes in many different forms, but most everyone feels it in some way. For me it can be people assuming my work ethic from how I look. For some people, it's fearing for their lives because of how they look, something that hurts my heart so badly. For some people, it's feeling left out of a clique at school or not interacting with the "cool kids." In our world it seems there are so many situations where we feel like we are judged for things we can't control.

John 1 tells us that, when Jesus came to the earth as a human (like us!), He was not received. It's hard for us when we feel unwelcome, and Jesus is right there with us. Imagine creating a world for the people you love, and them not receiving you when you come to live with them. It doesn't get much more unwelcoming than that!

So even when we feel unwelcome, we can know that the very God who created us knows exactly how we are feeling. Jesus knows us; and He knows what it's like to be unwelcome.

When you are feeling unwelcome you don't have to be afraid to invite Jesus into that with you. Jesus understands you, and He understands what you are going through.

People Like Me

In Luke 8, a woman is healed by Jesus, but I find the way she is healed to be so interesting. This woman did not feel worthy or comfortable enough to ask Jesus to heal her, so she snuck up behind Him while He was busy walking down a crowded street and touched his cloak.

How poorly must she have been treated for her to not even feel welcomed in the presence of Jesus? How badly hurt and disrespected was this woman that she wasn't able to directly confront the very man that she knew could heal her?

But what Jesus does with this is beautiful. He doesn't let her just walk away healed. He knows that she has been hurt and excluded for years, so Jesus acknowledges her presence.

I love the way that Jesus calls her out, too. After Jesus asks, "Who touched me?" the disciples tell Him that many people are touching Him, because the street is so crowded. But Jesus asks again.

Jesus knows who touched Him. Jesus knows why. But Jesus also knows that she hasn't been seen for who she is in a long time. She has only been seen for the dysfunction of her body, but no one has seen her for the beauty of her heart.

Jesus calls her out. In a good way! I love it. I love how after this woman spent the last twelve years of her life feeling unwelcome, Jesus didn't let her simply walk away with her miracle. Jesus was with her in her outcast-ness. He didn't tell her to change who she was or how she was, but He simply called out the part of her that made her a part of Him. Jesus called out the woman's faith, the part that connected her heart to His heart, but also the part of her that no one else noticed.

I feel unwelcome all the time. It's been a hard year for me, but I realize that Jesus comes to be with me in that place of feeling outcast. My Heavenly Father knows that I struggle with feeling different and alone, but my God doesn't shame me for that. Jesus meets me in it. Jesus calls out the parts of me that make me welcome in His heavenly home. God notices the things in my heart that connect me to Christ and make me a part of his family. So even though I still feel unwelcome, I also know that

God sees the parts of me that most people choose to overlook. I can be welcome in Christ even when I don't feel welcome in the world.

When you feel unwelcome, you are not alone.

Prayer

Take a deep breath. Know that God loves your heart, in any state it is in. So don't try and change your hurt on your own. Bring that pain to God and let the Holy Spirit into your heart. Pray the words you are able to pray right now, knowing that God delights in hearing your voice—even if it is only a few words.

God,

I'm so tired of feeling like nobody knows or understands who I really am on the inside. It feels like people only see me for my flaws, and my flaws make me feel like I stick out.

I want to be understood and welcomed for who I really am. I don't want to pretend to be something or someone I'm not.

Would You please remind me, even when I don't feel welcome anywhere in my life, that You will always see my heart and welcome me with open arms?

It's hard to remember sometimes that You love me no matter what when the people I'm surrounded by don't always do that.

Thank You for always being there for me.

I love You, Father. Amen.

When do you feel most unwelcome? When do you see other people feeling unwelcome? Talk to Jesus about those situations.

Section 3:

Exploring Your Emotions

What Are You Feeling? by Lucie Orozco

Hi, my name is Lucie Orozco and I'm the illustrator for this book! Helping make *The Emotional Devotional* was a really fun experience for me because I got to use what I've learned from almost three years of bullet journaling to create some of the activities you've seen here.

I have used bullet journaling mostly to keep track of some of my monthly habits and accomplishments. I also regularly use mood trackers to see how I am feeling from day to day. Basically, you can pick a shape or a theme and record where your mood is on a given day. It's not too complicated, but I wanted to give you a few examples to get you started.

Sometimes I pick a theme that goes with the month I'm in, so I'd be more likely to use plants or fish in the summer, raindrops in April, or jack-o'-lanterns in October.

I also like to add a key when I use different shapes or colors to represent each mood. I usually use a bunch of different colors (like in the Emotion Wheel on the front cover) or just different shades of the same color, depending on which looks best. Or sometimes I even just use some kind of graph to show where my feelings are headed this week.

There aren't any hard and fast rules. It's just a chance to record where you are and where you've been. It's easy to forget what you were feeling just a day or two ago, so I like to number my days as I go. And I try to record something at least once a day.

So here are a few options to get you started. You can use a variety of colors for the heart rays and the honeycomb, one for each color of the Emotion Wheel. For the citrus slices and records you might want to try different shades of the same color family to represent different emotions. I gave you some patterns to use on the books, and facial expressions for the ghosts, but everything is pretty much up to you!

These are just some suggestions, so see what works for you. Feel free to create your own, and thanks for being a part of this *Emotional Devotional*!

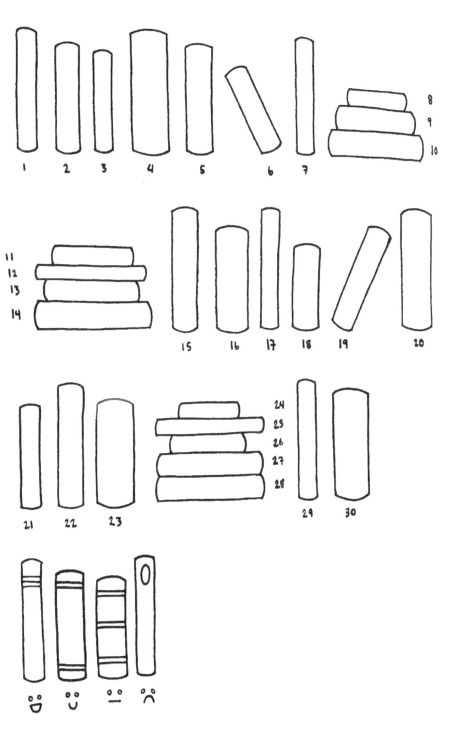

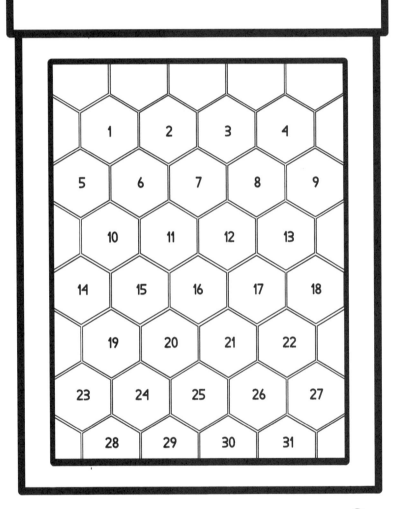

KEY:

MOODS

○ ○ ○ ○ ○

Explore Your Experience by Naomi Rossow

In this book, we talked about 36 different emotions. There are countless more emotions that humans experience (let alone teenagers!). Following this brief overview, you'll find some blank templates to help identify your own emotions and write about them. I love writing to figure out what I am feeling and talking to Jesus about what is going on in my life.

Try using these templates as an experiment. Invite Jesus to guide your heart throughout this process, and see if writing helps you identify and experience your emotions. Now, here's what to do with the templates.

1. Name Your Emotion

The first step to writing about your emotions is to figure out what emotions you are feeling. Back in Section 1, Gabriella gave a wonderful introduction on how to use the Emotion Wheel on the front cover of this book. That's an excellent tool to zoom in on the specific emotion you are feeling. You can also do a simple Google search to find a list of emotions or a different Emotion Wheel that may suit you better.

Start with the most generic emotions, like "angry" or "joyful." Then get more specific from there. You might not have the right word for what you are feeling; that's okay. You can still describe the emotion somehow. Remember that many emotions come in combinations, so it's okay to say you are Proud/Nervous or Exhausted/Grateful. Emotions are confusing and even conflicting at times. If you want, you can even make up a new name for what you're feeling! You aren't trying to get the "right answer". You are just trying to label your emotion in a way you would recognize. Having a name for your emotion allows you to feel it and process it in helpful ways.

After you have decided what emotion you want to write about, describe the emotion. This helps you to verify the emotion you are experiencing. It also gives you a chance to identify some emotional landmarks that can help you recognize this emotion in the future.

On a personal note: I found it helpful to include some other emotions that typically accompany the target emotion. Because we experience multiple emotions at once, this helps clear up some confusion that may come with assuming everything you're feeling is the product of a single emotion.

2. Listen to Your Body

One key part of the emotion description is to identify where you feel it in your body. Our body and mind are very interconnected. In times of severe stress and anxiety, your body produces adrenaline and prepares for either fight or flight. When you have been experiencing extreme emotions for a prolonged amount of time, you may get sick or extremely exhausted in response. Excitement can keep you up at night.

It's not just emotional extremes that get expressed in physical ways. It may be that all of your emotions have a home someplace in your body. Listen to what your body is telling you. Do your arms feel heavy? Are your cheeks red? Do your toes tingle? Is your stomach nervous, or sick, or full of butterflies? Where do you experience different emotions in different places in your body?

On a personal note: It can be hard at first to figure out what physical reactions and emotions go together. It is important to recognize that the same physical reaction may indicate a different emotion or vice versa. To help identify my personal physical reactions, I close my eyes and remember a time I felt a specific emotion. As I imagine myself in that emotion, I pay attention to the ghost of the physical symptoms in my present body.

3. Find a Bible Verse and People Like Me

The focus of this book is to follow Jesus in your emotions. Having a Bible verse about the emotion you are experiencing right now is a helpful guide to bringing Jesus into it. The Bible verse does not have to apply directly to you and your unique situation. If it had to apply exactly, we would never find one that did the job. In this book, we often tried to find a verse that explicitly named the emotion we were talking about. This helped focus the devotion on the emotion rather than getting distracted by the Bible story or other emotions involved.

As you search for a verse you are satisfied with, keep an open mind to other verses. There may be a perfect verse out there for your emotion, and there may only be an okay verse. Read multiple verses in multiple translations and invite Jesus to guide your mind to the right verse for you.

Finding a person from the Bible who experienced this emotion was also a helpful way of talking about the emotion. This allowed us to see that we are not the first people to experience the emotion and a reminder that we certainly won't be the last. The verse doesn't always come from the People Like Me story, but it very well can. If you are stuck, this could be a good way for you to expand your choices.

On a personal note: For almost every one of the Bible verses I found, I used the search tool on the Bible Gateway app. It allowed me to search an emotion by name and get results that both had the emotion in it and verses related to the emotion. You can also search more than one translation at the same time! Check it out at biblegateway.com.

4. Share Your Story

Sharing your unique story and your experience with the emotion gives you a chance to reflect on what happened with Jesus. This was my favorite part to write because I got to express my experiences and emotions in a way that was helpful to other girls as well as inviting them to see Jesus, even in their darkest times.

While I am usually pretty comfortable sharing my personal story, I know this is not the case for everyone. If you have trouble bringing others into your experiences, rest in the assurance that no one else has to read what you write unless you show it to them. Just like in the other sections, invite Jesus to be present in this experience. Ask the Holy Spirit to guide your heart and mind as you share your story.

On a personal note: While this was my favorite part, it was also the hardest part for me. If I got stuck while writing or couldn't come up with a good flow, I would take a few deep breaths and just write what I remembered. This allowed me to write without the pressure of having a format to the story. Just share your story. If you want, you can always go back and reformat it.

5. Invite Jesus

This book has been focused on bringing Jesus into your present emotion regardless of the circumstance around it. You don't need to "fix" your emotions, and there's no simple answer for how you should deal with them.

You can write out a simple, honest prayer expressing what you are feeling. Don't try to use only church words; just be yourself and talk like you. Jesus loves the real you, no matter what you are thinking or feeling right now.

If you aren't sure what to say, go back to Section 1 and try some of the Prayer Experiments there. Or make a list of words that are rattling around in your head and heart. Or draw a rough sketch of what you are feeling. Or copy some song lyrics that capture what you are feeling. Or write your own song. Or use prayers from the Bible as inspiration. (The Psalms are a great place to start!)

The point is, find some way to invite Jesus into what you are feeling. If you're stuck, pray: "Jesus, I don't know how to invite You into this, and I'm not sure I want to." Jesus is glad to hear that prayer. As you keep at it, turning your attention to Jesus in the midst of your emotions will start to seem normal. That habit will help you find your way forward with Jesus, even when your emotions seem confusing or out of control.

On a personal note: When I read the devotions in this book by these amazing girls that I love, it almost seems like they have it all together and are almost too good to be true. But I know them; and I know me. We aren't that good at this. We are struggling to find a way forward. We doubt, and we forget, and we fail. And Jesus is faithful. I can't tell you how many times my prayer life has been little more than, "Dear Jesus, Ahhhhhhh!!!!" And sometimes, it's not even that. But one thing I have learned, and keep learning: When you bring your emotions to Jesus, or invite Jesus into your emotions, it doesn't matter if you don't have it all together. It doesn't matter if you don't know what to say. It doesn't matter if you aren't faithful in prayer. Jesus is faithful. Always. And that's enough.

154

An Invitation

If you found any help or comfort reading about our experiences in this book, just imagine how other girls might benefit from hearing what Jesus is up to in *your* life! On this journey of faith, everyone has something to learn and something to share.

Email us your story at: communications@findmynextstep.org.

We follow Jesus better when we follow Him together, so we'll look for ways to share your story with other people. You can write about one of the emotions on our Emotion Wheel that we didn't cover or choose any emotion you want! It's up to you.

Use the templates provided or choose your own format or process. Run an experiment and see what works. But find some way to invite Jesus into your emotions. Jesus loves to be with you, whatever you are feeling!

My Emotion: _____

1. How I Experience this Emotion

What is it like? How does it feel? Where does it live in your body?

2. My Bible Verse

3. My Story

Write about a time you experienced this emotion.

4. People Like Me

Find a story in the Bible where a character experiences a similar emotion.

5. My Prayer

Invite Jesus into this emotion in your own words.

My Emotion: _____

How I Experience this Emotion

What is it like? How does it feel? Where does it live in your body?

My Bible Verse

My Story

Write about a time you experienced this emotion.

People Like Me

Find a story in the Bible where a character experiences a similar emotion.

My Prayer

Invite Jesus into this emotion in your own words.

My Emotion: _____

How I Experience this Emotion

What is it like? How does it feel? Where does it live in your body?

My Bible Verse

My Story

Write about a time you experienced this emotion.

People Like Me

Find a story in the Bible where a character experiences a similar emotion.

My Prayer

Invite Jesus into this emotion in your own words.

My Emotion: _____

How I Experience this Emotion

What is it like? How does it feel? Where does it live in your body?

My Bible Verse

My Story

Write about a time you experienced this emotion.

People Like Me

Find a story in the Bible where a character experiences a similar emotion.

My Prayer

Invite Jesus into this emotion in your own words.

About the Contributors

Naomi Rossow (19)

Introduction, Secure, Impatient, Defensive, Jealous, Celebration, Exhausted, Grief, Romantic, Doubtful, and Explore Your Experience

As a sophomore in college at Wayne State University in Detroit, Michigan, Naomi is finishing up her prerequisites and preparing to apply to nursing school. She loves volunteering at a clinic for pregnant moms and babies in downtown Detroit, and she has recently taken a position with a company that allows her to provide in-home care. She has published articles in the anthology *Jesus at the Center of My Messy Life: Tales from The Next Step Community, Year One* (2020) and continues to blog and create social media posts for her dad at Next Step Press. You can find more from Naomi at <u>community.findmynextstep.org</u>.

Gabriella Wiechman (18)

Introduction, Confident, Trusting, Grateful, Disconnected, Anticipation, Longing, Nervous, and Unwelcome

Inspired by her experiences in Uganda and El Salvador, Gabriella has begun to pursue a life in world missions. Civil unrest and COVID cancelled several mission trips for her in 2019 and 2020, so her training has been mostly in patience, endurance, unmet expectations, and inner transformation. She currently lives in Tomball, Texas with her family, working a lot with kids and blogging at <u>everyday4him.jimdofree.com</u>, where she inspires others to live their unique journey. She enjoys working out at her aunt's gym and making a mess in the kitchen. Gabriella is really looking forward to moving to Austin, Texas to become a full-time nanny as well as working at summer camp with her friends. She hopes this book will help young women notice and validate their emotions in the presence of their God who cares.

Elizabeth Rossow (17)

Prideful, Proud, Delight, Guilty, Failure, Hopeful, Empowered, and Uncertain

Liz opted for online school six months before COVID made online learning a common option. She is currently in her senior year of high school, but will delay graduation by a year so she can complete an early middle college program that will award her with an Associate's Degree from Baker College at the same time she gets her high school diploma. Her warm smile will greet you (from behind a mask) if you walk into the Panera in Brighton, Michigan, where she currently takes orders and runs food out to waiting vehicles. Liz enjoys reading and theatre and looks forward to acting with real live people again someday in the future.

Katherine Rossow (14)

Thoughtful, Frustrated, Triumphant, Awestruck, Inadequate, Trapped

Kate is an energetic eighthgrader who loves musical theatre, writing, fiction, and her family. She has a passion for helping people and hopes to teach, direct, and write someday as a career. She also loves sports, even though COVID has cancelled all athletics (at least for now). With in-person activities at a minimum, Kate has found ways to stay involved in online theatre productions, and keeps busy with her Instagram and TikTok accounts.

Eliana Wiechman (13)

Content, Carefree, Irritated, Lonely, Special

Ellie is an eighth-grade student in Tomball, Texas where she plays on the basketball team. She is the youngest of four siblings and treasures being around her friends and family. Ellie has a soft spot for animals (especially her cat, Covie), a passion for celebrating people (especially their birthdays), and a love of nature and beauty (especially mountains and flowers). Ellie enjoys playing her ukulele and singing at the top of her lungs in front of nobody in her room and making people feel special. She hopes these devotions will help girls know they are special to God.

Lucie Orozco (17)

What Are You Feeling? and all of the mood trackers and illustrations.

Lucie Orozco is a high school junior at Mott Middle College in Flint, Michigan, and first cousin to Naomi, Liz, and Kate. Lucie takes classes at the Flint Institute of Arts and plays the electric bass guitar in the worship band at her church. She loves to read in her free time and hopes to one day to be a professional illustrator.

About Next Step Press

Our Mission

Next Step Press cultivates individuals, leaders, and communities that infuse collaboration, innovation, and delight into the perpetual adventure of following Jesus. As part of that mission, we create resources that equip and encourage next step discipleship and support a culture of delight-driven discipleship growth.

Other Resources from Next Step Press

If you liked *The Emotional Devotional*, you might check out the following.

- *Delight! Discipleship as the Adventure of Loving and Being Loved.*
  This award-winning book from Justin Rossow helps you find renewed joy in the life of following Jesus.

- *Ponder Anew: A Hymn Journal of Trust and Confidence*
  Featuring illustrations from Visual Faith™ Ministry artists, this unique resource combines music, devotion, Scripture, art, and prayer.

- *Jesus at the Center of My Messy Life: Tales from the Next Step Community*
  The team of authors at community.findmynextstep.org share their stories and insights in refreshing ways that help you take a next step.

Made in United States
Troutdale, OR
04/14/2024

19169682R00100